1st Black President

The Race to the White House

by

Paula Diane Harris

authorHOUSE™

1663 LIBERTY DRIVE, SUITE 200
BLOOMINGTON, INDIANA 47403
(800) 839-8640
WWW.AUTHORHOUSE.COM

First published by AuthorHouse 09/15/04

ISBN: 1-4184-9990-0 (sc)
ISBN: 1-4184-9991-9 (dj)

Printed in the United States of America
Bloomington, Indiana

This book is printed on acid-free paper.

I dedicate this book to my daughter Rogette Nicole Harris who has been the inspiration in my life and the late Dr. Martin Luther King Jr., through his work and courage earned the respect of the human race and developed a leadership that has never been replaced in American History.

A special acknowledgement to Mr. Treff LamPlante

Table of Contents

Introduction

How do Black Americans become serious contenders for the highest office in the United States?

**"President Clinton was often known as the first black president",
Senator John Kerry of Massachusetts told the American Urban Radio
Network. "I wouldn't be upset if I could earn the right to be the
second".**

"1ˢᵗ Black President" is about how Black Americans must begin to obtain a **serious** role in American politics. In order to become a serious contender for the highest leadership position in America a black candidate must be taken seriously. Statements from Senator John Kerry, 2004 Democrat nominee for the President of the United States, confirm that black political candidates for president are not taken seriously and are overlooked as serious contenders for the presidency. This book discusses why black politicians support white candidates for president and gives examples of the type of black leadership that would be viewed as a serious candidate for the presidency.

This book will outline the requirements and qualifications for the office of the presidency. It will unravel how the Democrat Party has courted the Black vote taking their votes for granted. This book will discuss civil rights organizations and how black leadership has lost its focus and has managed to haul the civil rights movement in this country to become the token of the Democrat Party, selling out "Black America" for personal gains and their organizational role in American politics.

The country watched as two blacks ran for the Democrat Party nominee, Rev. Al Sharpton and Carol Mosley Braun in the 2004 primaries for president. In order to be taken seriously we must first identify Black Americans who will be respected as a **serious** contender for the White House based on their education, political experience and demeanor. This book will outline the education and experience an individual **must** master in order to become a serious contender by reviewing the qualifications of past presidents.

The divide and conquer slave mentality is alive and well and the sell out of civil rights by Black American leaders is just as dangerous to African Americans as the racist mentality of the KKK.

Black Americans who read this book will become challenged in the way they "think" about politics and their civil rights organizations but more importantly in how they see themselves. They will see the importance in recognizing when they are being taken for granted by politicians only to be used for their votes. There is only one America not two as John Edwards claims as he travels across the country. Blacks must not allow any voice to keep them segregated from the mainstream of America. Blacks must also realize that politicians are not concerned about our issues but rather only in being reelected; and they will use any group of people to succeed.

This book is a wake up call, if Black Americans want to become a serious contender for the highest leadership office of the United States; the presidency. It is a wake up call to bring the house slave and the field slave together joining forces to support one another ridding the plantation of Jim Crows and the Black American's who have used civil rights for their own personal gain, selling out their own people. Window dressing of civil rights must be eliminated and not used for political gain.

Paula Diane Harris, author tells the dynamic truth and gives solutions to Black Americans as the race to the White House continues.

Chapter I

Race to the White House

Kerry told the American Urban Radio Network: "President Clinton was often known as the first black president. I wouldn't be upset if I could earn the right to be the second."

John Kerry is not a black man — he is a privileged white man who has no idea what it is in this country to be a poor white, let alone a black. I asked Senator John Kerry to make a public apology for his statement in March 2004. Instead of Kerry apologizing for his statement knowing he had offended people his spokesman Chad Clanton made a statement. "This was intended as a light-natured remark about President Clinton's strong legacy with African Americans It is a legacy that John Kerry would like to build upon if elected president. John Kerry has a record of fighting for civil rights and as president he will continue this fight."

How can we believe that John Kerry will fight for the socially disadvantaged in this country when by his own statement it is evident John Kerry does not believe everyone is good enough to be his equal? Senator Kerry has been in the Senate for many years and he now wants to build on the legacy Clinton has had with blacks? Why now? I'll tell you why now. The Democrats need the black vote to win elections and Kerry's plan is to try and capitalize on Clinton's success with black voters. From his statement, Kerry's message was loud and clear. Blacks are not taken serious when

1

running to become the president of the United States but their votes are good enough for the Democrat Party.

Not one national civil rights leader in this country stood up against the statement. Instead because Kerry is a Democrat his statement was ignored. If a Republican made that remark the Urban League, NAACP, Rainbow Coalition and the Black Caucus would have had a press conference denouncing the statement and would have called for Kerry to step down for the racist remark. It is time for Black Americans to wake up and accept the fact that blacks are not taken serious in politics and they are taken for granted in the Democrat Party.

Civil rights leaders give the perception that they only care about their personal gains selling off black issues. How sad for those who paved the way, who paid the ultimate sacrifice; for those who have given their lives for justice and equality only to have been sold out by the current black leadership in this country.

Black voters must recognize that it is no longer the political party that should capture their loyalties but rather the focus must be on the candidate. America's diversity of its people cannot afford to have a president who does not believe that all men and women have equal constitutional rights and protection. All Americans are born with the right to obtain equal opportunities regardless of their economic status, race or religion.

Many Black Americans have been led to believe that if Democrat nominee John Kerry is the best we can do then as long as we get Bush out of the White House we will settle with John Kerry. A good analogy of this would be is for women to settle for a man that doesn't work and who won't take responsibility for his children as long as they have a man. This way of thinking is no more in your best interest then accepting a politician who clearly does not see you as their equal.

As citizens, it is time that the American village raises its standards for the politicians we choose to represent us. I admit that President Bush has made his mistakes but whether people agree or disagree he doesn't flip flop on his positions, and that I can deal with. The Democrat Party had a chance to elect a nominee to become the alternative to George W. Bush but they missed the opportunity with John Kerry as the nominee. Democrat presidential candidate John Kerry missed most of the public hearings of the Senate Intelligence Committee during his eight years on the panel according to his colleagues. During his eight year tenure on the committee, which provides oversight of national intelligence agencies, Kerry was absent for 38 of 49 public hearings, according to Sen. Saxby Chambliss, R-Georgia. This alone should be a great concern with the problems the US is having with intelligence. How can we not ask the question based on his attendance record in the Senate will John Kerry take his responsibilities serious and be on the job if he is elected president?

There's been a total avoidance of discussion of the voting record of John Kerry by the media. American voters need to be asking why?

No president is able to please all of the people all of the time however, due to America's diversity we need a leader to recognize that they must

represent all of the people **equally** all of the time and that goes for George
W. Bush as well as Senator John Kerry.

Qualifications

The Constitution requires that a candidate for the presidency must be
a "natural-born" citizen of the United States, at least 35 years of age, and a
resident of the United States for at least 14 years. If you think this gives all
the requirements needed to win the highest office, think again. This is all
you need to run as a candidate. We will explore in this chapter a complete
picture of a serious candidate for president.

Senator John Kerry made it clear in his remark to the American Urban
Radio Network that as Black Americans we have a long way to go before we
will be seen as a serious candidate for president.

Before we begin our journey many people have different terms in
describing "Black American's" depending on the generation as well as the
preference of the speaker. But for clarity whether or not you use **Black**
Americans, **Afro** Americans, or **African** Americans the definitions are all the
same they mean an American whose ancestors were born in Africa

Neither, Senator Kerry or Former President Bill Clinton would qualify
to be considered a Black American President. Why? Neither one of these
men are black! It is very troubling to me that blacks were responsible in
labeling Bill Clinton as the first Black President of the United States. Blacks'
who accept and ignore this statement give the perception that we are not

capable in becoming the President of the United States. What message does this give our children? Doing so is admitting to the world that our children cannot aspire and achieve leadership in a country where their ancestors in slavery helped to build. Ignoring these type of statements to go unchallenged is self- destructive for our people and more importantly for our children. Senator Kerry's statement was unacceptable and indicates a clear disrespect that in his thinking Black Americans will never accomplish this role in being elected to the highest leadership position in this nation. What is even more troubling is when it was brought to his attention that he offended people he didn't think it was important enough to apologize.

As qualified blacks struggle to obtain middle management positions many of them over qualified with their education and experience, we must demand respect. In many instances Black are still overlooked for top and mid level management positions across this nation. Employment discrimination is at its highest form in America. However, you don't hear much about it until politicians are running for elected positions. These are the type of issues civil rights organizations need to be fighting instead of calling all Republicans names just to get attention at their outdated annual convention as Julian Bond did last month.

When riots erupted in many American cities in the 1960s, many newspaper editors and TV executives had few, if any, journalists or broadcasters of color to send into burning neighborhoods and downtowns to cover the story.

This problem does not exist today becuase there are more than 8,100 black, Hispanic, Asian and Native American journalists and broadcasters in the United States. Despite these impressive numbers, the number of minorities in the mainstream news media still doesn't represent the nation's growing ethnic population

Statements such as John Kerry's will continue to hold Black's at the back of the bus in employment opportunities. If we as a people don't believe in ourselves and in our children then who else will? We must raise our standards and not believe that we have to be content with less then we are worth. Most importantly, there are black children who aspire to become the President of these United States. They are American citizens and have the right to try and seek the office of the presidency with dignity and respect. Black Americans helped build this country, they helped defend it in war and they place their lives on the line as secret service agents protecting the lives of politicians like Senator John Kerry.

The race to the White House is more then just a presidential election for Black Americans. It is about finding and implementing solutions to a 21st century political slavery trap for Blacks as we tap into the process of elect-ability for Black Americans to be taken serious as a presidential candidate.

An understanding of our nation's government process is essential for the role of President. The framers of the Constitution believed that a person must be born in the United States in order to understand the country. Today we have problems in public education where many children are fighting to obtain an equal quality public education. Unfortunately, being a natural born citizen doesn't guarantee an equal, quality education for every child.

Thomas Jefferson was a champion of universal education for all citizens, but in the culture in which he wrote, black slaves were not considered citizens. Jefferson saw the institution of slavery as an evil, even though he continued the practice of slave ownership. Jefferson's own contradictory actions toward his slaves were symbolic of the paradox that would describe race relations and equality in education for Black Americans. The nation would have to suffer through a bloody civil war and over one hundred years of racial strife to arrive at a time when a more equitable education would be available to all Americans. Still today in many school districts across the nation an equal, quality education has not been accomplished for the socially disadvantaged.

Brown v. Board of Education

The landmark Supreme Court case of Brown v. Board of Education (1954) settled the question of whether or not blacks and Whites will receive an education integrated with or separate from each other. The case overturned the 1896 case of Plessy v. Ferguson, which established the doctrine of "separate but equal." This concept stated that separate public facilities of equal quality do not violate the equal protection clause of the Fourteenth Amendment of the Constitution, which reads:

Section 1. All persons born or naturalized in the United States, and subject to the jurisdiction thereof, are citizens of the United States and of the state wherein they reside. No state shall make or enforce any law, which shall abridge the privileges or immunities of citizens of the United States; nor shall any state deprive any person of life, liberty, or property, without due process of law; nor deny to any person within its jurisdiction the equal protection of the laws.

Linda Brown was an eight year old, black child who had to cross Topeka, Kansas to attend grade school, while her white friends were able to attend classes at a public school a few blocks away. The Topeka School system was segregated on the basis of race, and under the separate but equal doctrine, this arrangement was acceptable and legal. Linda's parents sued in federal district court on the basis that separate facilities for blacks were innately unequal. The lower courts agreed with the school system that if the facilities were equal, the child was being treated equal with whites as prescribed by the Fourteenth Amendment. The Browns and other families in other school systems appealed to the Supreme Court that even facilities that were physically equal did not take into account "intangible" factors, and that segregation itself has a deleterious effect on the education of black children. Their case was encouraged by the National Association for the Advancement of Colored People (NAACP) and was argued before the Supreme Court by Thurgood Marshall, who would later become the first black justice on the Supreme Court.

I don't believe Mr. Marshall if he were with us today having had accomplished being the first black justice in the Supreme Court would have saw humor in Senator Kerry's remark nor would he have understood how the NAACP sat by in silence. This couldn't be the same NAACP that encouraged the Browns case before the Supreme Court? A civil rights organization that's leadership has become the token of the Democrat Party whose interest is in obtaining memberships where in most are inactive across the nation. Their focus being on their annual Image Awards where the memberships have no voice in who obtains these awards. The NAACP's annual conventions that continue to lead black dollars to be spent in white hotels and businesses each year without solutions to such issues as employment has failed to assist local branches financially. An organization that is outdated where a large ineffective membership has no voice in voting in the Chairman or President and CEO. It is crime in the national office that in 2004 many local branches are still operating in homes. Many branches are without fax machines or computers and because of the inactivity of local memberships ineffective branch leaderships are elected in communities unable to voice the issues. You only have to be a member 180 days to be elected as a branch president. That's the qualifications and in today's world it is not enough to be qualified to handle the issues.

In order to be respected you have to respect yourself and stand on principal as they did with the landmark Supreme Court case of Brown v. Board of Education (1954). It didn't matter who was Democrat or Republican. What mattered was the issue of segregation regarding public education for blacks. Much is being discussed about the changing of the guard in the white house but a true fact remains and that is it is time for a new leadership in the black house representing civil rights as it should, not window dressing it for personal gain.

35 Years of Age

Personal experience was important to those who framed the requirements of the presidency. They felt that unless a person had reached age thirty-five, it was doubtful for that person to have experienced enough to govern a nation.

Although many Americans are distrustful of government, wary of the news media and disinterested in politics, they resoundingly endorse the economic and democratic systems on which the nation is grounded. When looking back on the accomplishments of the 20th century, overwhelming majorities agree that the Constitution (85%), free elections (84%), and the free enterprise system (81%) are major reasons for the success that the U.S. has enjoyed during the past 100 years. The public seems frustrated by how the system operates, but they accept the design.

In addition, despite Americans' increasing skepticism about press practices, more than two-thirds of the public (69%) credits national success to freedom of the press. A similar majority also gives credit to divine sources: 65% say God's will is a major reason for American success.

Today by the time the average individual completes their education obtaining a masters degree or PHD, runs for a state level elected office then a national level elected office or is appointed by a current president in a cabinet position, they would be 35 years or older. John Fitzgerald Kennedy was America's youngest elected President; he was also the youngest to die at age 43.

14-Year Residency

Part of being President involves dealing with both domestic and foreign problems. In order to face these problems, previous knowledge of the nation's history in these matters is necessary. The framers decided that fourteen years was an adequate time span to comprehend these issues.

A child born to citizen parents living overseas is in fact a "natural born Citizen of the United States." If the child meets other eligibility requirements (particular the 14 year residency requirement), he or she can hold the office of President. (Incidentally, there was some controversy about whether or not Eisenhower had met the 14-year requirement before assuming the presidency because he had lived outside the country for an extended period of time as a military commander during the 14 years immediately preceding his bid for the Oval Office. The conclusion in his case was that the 14 years did not have to be consecutive.

All other offices under the Constitution are open to citizens, both natural born and naturalized

The words "natural born" means persons born citizens of the United States are considered natural-born. Therefore, a child born of illegal immigrants or born on U.S. soil yet lived his or her life out of the nation could still be President. A naturalized citizen could not.

Also, a person does not have to be married. There have been several Presidents who were not married at the time of their election or during their term of office.

The president of the United States is considered the head of the Executive Branch of government and is also viewed as the leader of the United States government. While the president does have significant power, their power is limited by the constitution. A good example is the Iraq war. Many people blame our current President George W. Bush for the Iraq War on terrorism thinking he was solely responsible for the decision in America going to war. According to the constitution, the president would not have been able to enter the United States into war without the vote of the United States Congress.

Section 8 of the United States Constitution, the Congress has the power to declare war **NOT** the president. The constitution was written defining duties of the president and the congress to prevent one person having all the power that leads to dictatorship. Between Congress having the right to declare war they also have the powers to set and collect taxes, duties, imposts and excises, to pay the debts and provide for the common defense and general welfare of the United States; but all duties, imposts and excises shall be uniform throughout the United States; To borrow money on the credit of the United States; To regulate commerce with foreign nations, and between the several states, and with the Indian tribes; To establish a uniform rule of naturalization, and uniform laws on the subject of bankruptcies throughout the United States; To coin money, regulate the value thereof, and of foreign coin, and fix the standard of weights and measures; To provide for the punishment of counterfeiting the securities and current coin of the United States; To establish post offices and post roads; To promote the progress of science and useful arts, by securing for limited times to authors and inventors the exclusive right to their respective writings and discoveries; To constitute tribunals inferior to the Supreme Court; To define and punish piracies and felonies committed on the high seas, and offenses against the law of nations; To **declare war**, grant letters of marquee and reprisal, and **make rules concerning captures on land and water;** To **raise and support armies**, but no appropriation of money to that use shall be for a longer term than two years; To **provide and maintain a navy;** To **make rules for the government and regulation of the land and naval forces**; To **provide for calling forth the militia to execute the laws of the union, suppress insurrections and repel invasions;** To provide for organizing, arming, and disciplining, the militia, and for governing part of them as may be employed in the service of the United States, reserving to the states respectively, the appointment of the officers, and the authority of training the militia according to the discipline prescribed by Congress.

To exercise exclusive legislation in all cases over such districts (not exceeding ten miles square) as may, by cession of particular states, and the acceptance of Congress, become the seat of the government of the United States, and to exercise like authority over all places purchased by the consent of the legislature of the state in which the same shall be, for the erection of forts, magazines, arsenals, dockyards, and other needful buildings—And

To make all laws, this shall be necessary and proper for carrying into execution the foregoing powers, and all other powers, vested by this

Constitution in the government of the United States, or in any department or officer thereof.

296 Democrats and Republicans voted to authorize the use of the United States Armed Forces against Iraq. It was their job as representatives of the people to ensure there was a plan if we went to war. It was their job to guarantee against risk that there was enough evidence of weapons of mass destruction. Congress did not do their job representing the American people and they should be replaced both Democrats and Republicans those who voted yes.

The president did not and could not have acted alone. Congress gave President George W. Bush the power and should be held equally responsible. This is a major problem I have with Senator John Kerry who has now flipped flopped on the war and had the same intelligence information as the president had when making the decision for war. Now that there are problems in Iraq and Kerry is running for president he wants to distance himself and cover up his voting record in the United States Senate. America needs leadership that will stand firm even when decisions are made that perhaps are not popular with voters. We cannot afford flip-flopping over issues just to be popular. There are going to be times just as in raising children the decisions made are not the ones we want to hear but they are in our best interest. If a mistake is made, own up to the American people and learn from the mistake so we can get it corrected. This is a message for President Bush and Senator John Kerry.

This is how the United States Congress voted giving the president the power therefore making them **equally** responsible for the war in Iraq and the problems and issues surrounding the war:

FINAL VOTE RESULTS FOR ROLL CALL 455

H J RES 114 YEA-AND-NAY 10-OCT-2002 3:05 PM

QUESTION: On Passage

BILL TITLE: To Authorize the Use of United States Armed Forces against Iraq.

	Yeas	Nays	PRES	NV
Republican	215	6		2
Democratic	81	126		1
Independent		1		
TOTALS	**296**	**133**		**3**

Due to the attack on September 11, 2001 our country was bleeding due to the thousands of American lives lost. Those who voted "yes" to give President Bush the power for the war in Iraq must be held equally responsible for the outcome. At the time in my opinion politicians who voted yes were thinking of themselves and their re-elections. They were afraid that if they voted against the war their constituents would not re-elect them because of 911. This is why it is important to be educated on how the political system works and primarily the branches of government.

The constitution assigns the following powers to the president:

- Commander in Chief of the armed Forces
- Make treaties, with two-thirds consent of the Senate
- Receive ambassadors and other public ministers from foreign countries
- Appoints ambassadors, Supreme Court Justices, federal judges, and any officials provided for by the Congress, with the approval of the Senate
- Give an annual state of the union address to the Congress.
- Recommend legislation to the Congress
- Convene Congress on extraordinary occasions
- Adjourn Congress in cases of disagreement about adjournment
- Clearly understand the laws that they are executed successful
- Fill in administration vacancies during Congressional recesses.
- Grant reprieves and pardons for offences against the United States

The President and the Vice President are the only officials elected by the entire country. When elected the president serves a term of four years not more then two terms. This is identified as term limits. Before 1951 the President was able to serve as many terms as they were elected. Nevertheless, every President followed George Washington's example of stepping down after two terms. President Franklin D. Roosevelt changed tradition. Roosevelt successfully ran for office four times. Early in his fourth term, in 1945 he died. Six years later, Congress passed the 22nd Amendment that limits the president to two terms. If the president of the United States has term limits so should every other level of elected officials from local levels through the senate.

Term limits allows for new representation and protects elected officials from gaining too much power over people thus resulting in dictatorship. Term limits also rids our political systems of career politicians who use the system to their own advantage not serving the people who elect them. Power and money are human beings greatest downfall and resources of evil. The more they obtain the more they want. Elected officials who obtain political power and misuses it, placing individuals, companies and organizations in political slavery, in bondage. This behavior is a threat to our freedoms and democracy and is not what public servants were created to do. I have seen this on local, county and state levels from elected officials.

Temptation of political power is great and term limits would allow voters to fire these types of controlling personalities ridding them out of our political system. Remember, the way to fire a public official is at the voting polls or as California accomplished with former Governor Davis with a recall election. It is unfortunate that hardly any other states have recall elections within their state constitutions. In most situations in order to fire an elected official it must be done at the polls during elections. Political officials on all levels work for the people. We hire them and we have the power when we use our democracy voice at the polls to fire them or not hire them.

Electable Candidate Selection Process

The qualifications to become the President of the United States and
the powers assigned to the President as we reviewed are two different areas
of needed requirements. In order to become a serious black candidate it
is unlikely that you will succeed in being taken serious if you do not have
both areas of qualifications. Therefore, do yourself and Black Americans
a favor; first master the qualifications before you run because you will
not be taken seriously otherwise. It takes more then a 'good' speech for a
Black American to become a serious candidate for the presidency of the
United States. As in many leadership positions if you are considered socially
disadvantaged you almost have to be over qualified to be a serious contender
for a leadership position where you would oversee white employees. A
good example is corporate America. There are managers and there are
project managers. Project managers and analysts are given specific projects
that they are accountable for and do not usually supervise employees.
Directors, managers and supervisors considered middle management
oversee employees as their superiors. It is very difficult for a black to be
selected in these employment areas over whites. Companies who try and sell
their diversity and affirmative action policies place white females in these
positions over blacks. Another employment area Black Americans are placed
is human resource and employee relation positions. Blacks are placed in
these positions without any power where they themselves report to white
superiors. This gives a company the perception that the company is diverse
in its policies and equal treatment of employment opportunities when in
reality they are just window dressing. Black Americans when hired in these
positions understandably, feel empowered even though they realize that they

are in many instances powerless to either hire or promote other non-whites. The selection process in where they hire Black Americans is interesting. In American slavery how did the white master choose who worked in the house and who worked in the field? In today's corporate plantation in America how do they decide who works in the mailroom and who works in the human resource office when the individuals have the same qualifications?

Jim Crow laws worked in the 1800's and they still work today; same techniques different plantation. From the 1880s into the 1960s, a majority of American states enforced segregation through "Jim Crow" laws. These laws were named after a black character in minstrel show. From Delaware to California, and from North Dakota to Texas, many states (and cities, too) were able to impose legal punishments on people for consorting with members of another race. The most common types of laws forbade intermarriage and ordered business owners and public institutions to keep their black and white clientele separated.

Today Black Americans are faced with the same issues. We continue to see the creation of Jim Crow techniques through employment discrimination, housing, financing, and credit ratings and in other forms. Many blacks continue struggling to survive the Jim Crow ghost in their lives, the Jim Crow that at times look like us. Unfortunately, these techniques that were once used to keep Blacks in line have begun to be used by Blacks and civil rights organizations selling each other out like the Africans who sold their people into American slavery. I witnessed and experience this when I was NAACP local President. I used to say that the white master wouldn't have known what was going on in the village unless one of us told it! These type of Black Americans are just as dangerous as members of the KKK. The transition from segregation to civil rights lost its purpose when we lost our leader Dr. Martin Luther King Jr. Instead those who tried to replace him were bought and tied up by the modern Jim Crows who found their price and bought their souls. The first Black American President of these United States must be a leader that won't give into their price tag hanging from his or her check book selling off the cross of equality, justice and freedoms. The first Black American President will understand the dream that was left and will work towards making it a reality for all people.

In order to be a serious Black contender for the presidency the individual must overcome the huge obstacle and that is the stereotype perception of Black Americans in this country. This is explained later in Chapter "Blacks Don't Read". It is unfortunate that the perception in America regarding Blacks in some cases is deserved but in many cases not deserved.

To become the President of the United States you must first obtain the nomination of one of the major political parties, the Republicans or Democrats. This is not easy for a white male to achieve and has never been achieved by a Black American. You would think that the first Black President would be a Democrat because a high percentage of Black Americans are registered Democrats but when you review the inside of the National Democrat Committee leadership positions paid and non-paid it is not as diverse as they lead the public to believe. Even though the Democrats try and give the perception that they represent the middle class know for a fact that the leaderships within the Democrat Party are just as rich and privileged as in the Republican Party. There are no middle class Americans running either party only the rich and the richer. This falls right in line with the message" President Clinton was often known as the first black president, Senator John Kerry of Massachusetts told the American Urban Radio Network. "I wouldn't be upset if I could earn the right to be the second". The insult continued when Kerry's spokesman Chad Clanton said" this was intended as a light natured remark about President Clinton's strong legacy with Black Americans." No apology from Senator Kerry even though he was aware his remark offended people. How can Black Americans vote for a person who doesn't respect them as their equal?

Many Black Americans are tired in being a light natured joke in this country and our votes taken for granted. Throughout this book you will read many others who emailed me their feelings regarding Senator Kerry's remark from across the nation.

A review of qualifications of Past Presidents

We have reviewed and understand the qualifications and requirements of the presidency and their powers. In order to help recognize a qualified Black American candidate who would be taken serious if he or she would become a candidate, let us now review the education and experience of past elected presidents who were all white males. The Black American candidate for president who will be taken **serious** must strive to accomplish the same standards of education and experience of our past presidents.

Past elected Presidents are in alphabetical order

John Adams 1797-1801

John Adams was more of a political philosopher than a politician. "People and nations are forged in the fires of adversity," he said, doubtless thinking of his own as well as the American experience.

Adams was born in the Massachusetts Bay Colony in 1735. **A Harvard-educated lawyer**, he early became identified with the patriot cause; a delegate to the First and Second Continental Congresses, he led in the movement for independence.

During the Revolutionary War he **served in France and Holland in diplomatic roles**, and helped negotiate the treaty of peace. From 1785 to 1788 he was **minister to the Court of St. James's**, returning to be **elected Vice President under George Washington.**

John Quincy Adams 1825-29

The first President who was the **son of a President**, John Quincy Adams in many respects paralleled the career as well as the temperament and viewpoints of his illustrious father. Born in Braintree, Massachusetts, in 1767, he watched the Battle of Bunker Hill from the top of Penn's Hill above the family farm. As **secretary to his father** in Europe, he became an **accomplished linguist and assiduous diarist.**

After **graduating from Harvard College, he became a lawyer**. At age 26 he was **appointed Minister to the Netherlands, and then promoted to the Berlin Legation**. In **1802 he was elected to the United States Senate**. Six years later **President Madison appointed him Minister to Russia.**

Serving under President Monroe, Adams was one of **America's great Secretaries of State**, arranging with England for the joint occupation of the Oregon country, obtaining from Spain the cession of the Florida's, and formulating with the President the Monroe Doctrine.

Chester A. Arthur 1881-85

Dignified, tall, and handsome, with clean-shaven chin and side-whiskers, Chester A. Arthur "looked like a President."

The **son of a Baptist preacher** who had emigrated from Northern Ireland, Arthur was born in Fairfield, Vermont, in 1829. He was **graduated from Union College in 1848, taught school, was admitted to the bar,** and practiced law in New York City. Early in the Civil War he **served as Quartermaster General of the State of New York.**

President Grant in 1871 **appointed him Collector of the Port of New York**. Arthur **effectively marshaled the thousand Customs House employees under his supervision on behalf of Roscoe Conkling's**

Stalwart Republican machine.

James Buchanan 1857-61

Tall, stately, stiffly formal in the high stock he wore around his jowls, James Buchanan was the **only President who never married.**

Presiding over a rapidly dividing Nation, Buchanan grasped inadequately the political realities of the time. Relying on constitutional doctrines to close the widening rift over slavery, he failed to understand that the North would not accept constitutional arguments, which favored the South. Nor could he realize how sectionalism had realigned political parties: the Democrats split; the Whigs were destroyed, giving rise to the Republicans.

Born into a well-to-do Pennsylvania family in 1791, Buchanan, a graduate of Dickinson College, was gifted as a debater and learned in the law.

He was **elected five times to the House of Representatives, and then served for s decade to the Senate.**

George Bush 1989-93

George Bush brought to the White House a dedication to traditional American values and a determination to direct them toward making the United States "a kinder and gentler nation." In his Inaugural Address he pledged in "a moment rich with promise" to use American strength as "a force for good."

Coming from a family with a tradition of public service, George Herbert Walker Bush felt the responsibility to make his contribution both in time of war and in peace. Born in Milton, Massachusetts, on June 12, 1924, he became a **student leader at Phillips Academy in Andover**. On his **18th birthday he enlisted in the armed forces**. The youngest pilot in the Navy when he received his wings, he **flew 58 combat missions during World War II.** On one mission over the Pacific as a torpedo bomber pilot he was shot down by Japanese antiaircraft fire and was rescued from the water by a U. S. submarine. He was awarded the Distinguished Flying Cross for bravery in action.

Bush next turned his energies toward completing his education and raising a family. In January 1945 he married Barbara Pierce

President George W. Bush 2001-present

George W. Bush is the 43rd President of the United States. He was sworn into office January 20, 2001, after a campaign in which he outlined sweeping proposals to reform America's public schools, transform our national defense, provide tax relief, modernize Social Security and Medicare, and encourage faith-based and community organizations to work with government to help Americans in need. President **Bush served for six years as the 46th Governor of the State of Texas**, where he earned a reputation as a compassionate conservative who shaped public policy based on the principles of limited government, personal responsibility, strong families, and local control.

President Bush was born on July 6, 1946, in New Haven, Connecticut, and he grew up in Midland and Houston, Texas. **He received a bachelor's degree from Yale University in 1968, and then served as an F-102 fighter pilot in the Texas Air National Guard**. President Bush **received a Master of Business Administration from Harvard Business School in 1975**. After graduating, he moved back to Midland and began a career in the energy business. After working on his father's successful 1988 presidential campaign, he assembled the group of partners that purchased the Texas Rangers baseball franchise in 1989.

Jimmy Carter 1977-81

Jimmy Carter aspired to make Government "competent and compassionate," responsive to the American people and their expectations. His achievements were notable, but in an era of rising energy costs, mounting inflation, and continuing tensions, it was impossible for his administration to meet these high expectations.

Carter, who has rarely used his full name—James Earl Carter, Jr.—, was born October 1, 1924, in Plains, Georgia. **Peanut farming**, talk of politics, and **devotion to the Baptist faith** were mainstays of his upbringing. Upon **graduation in 1946 from the Naval Academy in Annapolis, Maryland**, Carter married Rosalynn Smith. The Carters have three sons, John William (Jack), James Earl III (Chip), Donnel Jeffrey (Jeff), and a daughter, Amy Lynn.

After **seven years' service as a naval officer**, Carter returned to Plains. In 1962 he **entered state politics**, and **eight years later he was elected Governor of Georgia**. Among the new young southern governors, he attracted attention by emphasizing ecology, efficiency in government, and the removal of racial barriers.

Grover Cleveland 1885-89, 1893-97

The First Democrat elected after the Civil War, Grover Cleveland was the only President to leave the White House and return for a second term four years later.

One of nine children of a Presbyterian minister, Cleveland was born in New Jersey in 1837. He was raised in upstate New York. As **a lawyer** in Buffalo, he became notable for his single-minded concentration upon whatever task faced him.

At 44, he emerged into a political prominence that carried him to the White House in three years. Running as a reformer, he was **elected Mayor of Buffalo in 1881 and later, Governor of New York**

William J. Clinton 1993-2001

During the administration of William Jefferson Clinton, the U.S. enjoyed more peace and economic well being than at any time in its history. He was the first Democratic president since Franklin D. Roosevelt to win a second term. He could point to the lowest unemployment rate in modern times, the lowest inflation in 30 years, the highest home ownership in the country's history, dropping crime rates in many places, and reduced welfare roles. He proposed the first balanced budget in decades and achieved a budget surplus. As part of a plan to celebrate the millennium in 2000, Clinton called for a great national initiative to end racial discrimination.

After the failure in his second year of a huge program of health care reform, Clinton shifted emphasis, declaring, "The era of big government is over." He sought legislation to upgrade education, to protect jobs of parents who must care for sick children, to restrict handgun sales, and to strengthen environmental rules.

President Clinton was born William Jefferson Blythe IV on August 19, 1946, in Hope, Arkansas, three months after his father died in a traffic accident. When he was four years old, his mother wed Roger Clinton, of Hot Springs, Arkansas. In high school, he took the family name.

He **excelled as a student** and as a saxophone player and once considered becoming a professional musician. As a delegate to Boys Nation while in high school, he met President John Kennedy in the White House Rose Garden. The encounter led him to enter a life of public service.

Clinton graduated from Georgetown University and in 1968 won a Rhodes scholarship to Oxford University. He received a law degree from Yale University in 1973, and entered politics in Arkansas.

Calvin Coolidge 1923-29

At 2:30 on the morning of August 3, 1923, while visiting in Vermont, Calvin Coolidge received word that he was President. By the light of a kerosene lamp, his father, who was a notary public, administered the oath of office as Coolidge placed his hand on the family Bible.

Coolidge was "distinguished for character more than for heroic achievement," wrote a Democratic admirer, Alfred E. Smith. "His great task was to restore the dignity and prestige of the Presidency when it had reached the lowest ebb in our history … in a time of extravagance and waste…."

Born in Plymouth, Vermont, on July 4, 1872, Coolidge was the son of a village storekeeper. **He was graduated from Amherst College with honors, and entered law and politics in Northampton, Massachusetts.** Slowly, methodically, **he went up the political ladder from councilman in Northampton to Governor of Massachusetts**, as a Republican. En route he became thoroughly conservative.

Dwight D. Eisenhower 1953-61

Bringing to the Presidency his prestige as commanding general of the victorious forces in Europe during World War II, Dwight D. Eisenhower obtained a truce in Korea and worked incessantly during his two terms to ease the tensions of the Cold War. He pursued the moderate policies of "Modern Republicanism," pointing out as he left office, "America is today the strongest, most influential, and most productive nation in the world."

Born in Texas in 1890, brought up in Abilene, Kansas, Eisenhower was the third of seven sons. **He excelled in sports in high school, and received an appointment to West Point. Stationed in Texas as a second lieutenant**, he met Mamie Geneva Doud, whom he married in 1916.

In his early Army career, he excelled in staff assignments, serving under Generals John J. Pershing, Douglas MacArthur, and Walter Krueger. After Pearl Harbor, General George C. Marshall called him to Washington for a war plans assignment. He commanded the Allied Forces landing in North Africa in November 1942; on D-Day, 1944, he was Supreme Commander of the troops invading France.

After the war, he **became President of Columbia University**, and then took leave to **assume supreme command over the new NATO forces** being assembled in 1951. Republican emissaries to his headquarters near Paris persuaded him to run for President in 1952.

Millard Fillmore 1850-53

In his rise from a log cabin to wealth and the White House, Millard Fillmore demonstrated that through methodical industry and some competence an uninspiring man could make the American dream come true.

Born in the Finger Lakes country of New York in 1800, Fillmore as a youth endured the privations of frontier life. He **worked on his father's farm**, and **at 15 was apprenticed to a cloth dresser**. He attended one-room schools, and fell in love with the redheaded teacher, Abigail Powers, who later became his wife.

In 1823 he was admitted to the bar; seven years later he moved his law practice to Buffalo. **As an associate of the Whig politician Thurlow Weed, Fillmore held state office and for eight years was a member of the House of Representatives. In 1848, while Comptroller of New York, he was elected Vice President.**

Fillmore presided over the Senate during the months of nerve-wracking debates over the Compromise of 1850. He made no public comment on the merits of the compromise proposals, but a few days before President Taylor's death, he intimated to him that if there should be a tie vote on Henry Clay's bill, he would vote in favor of it.

Gerald R. Ford 1974-77

When Gerald R. Ford took the oath of office on August 9, 1974, he declared, "I assume the Presidency under extraordinary circumstances…. This is an hour of history that troubles our minds and hurts our hearts."

It was indeed an unprecedented time. He had been the **first Vice President chosen under the terms of the Twenty-fifth Amendment and, in the aftermath of the Watergate scandal, was succeeding the first President ever to resign.**

Ford was confronted with almost insuperable tasks. There were the challenges of mastering inflation, reviving a depressed economy, solving chronic energy shortages, and trying to ensure world peace.

Ford's reputation for integrity and openness had made him popular during his 25 years in Congress. From 1965 to 1973, he was House Minority Leader. Born in Omaha, Nebraska, in 1913, he grew up in Grand Rapids, Michigan. **He starred on the University of Michigan football team, and then went to Yale, where he served as assistant coach while earning his law degree. During World War II he attained the rank of lieutenant commander in the Navy. After the war he returned to Grand Rapids, where he began the practice of law,** and entered Republican politics

James A. Garfield 1881

As the last of the log cabin Presidents, James A. Garfield attacked political corruption and won back for the Presidency a measure of prestige it had lost during the Reconstruction period.

He was born in Cuyahoga County, Ohio, in 1831. **Fatherless at two, he later drove canal boat teams, somehow earning enough money for an education. He was graduated from Williams College in Massachusetts in 1856,** and he **returned to the Western Reserve Eclectic Institute (later Hiram College) in Ohio as a classics professor. Within a year he was made its president.**

Garfield was elected to the Ohio Senate in 1859 as a Republican. During the secession crisis, he advocated coercing the seceding states back into the Union.

In 1862, when Union military victories had been few, he successfully led a brigade at Middle Creek, Kentucky, against Confederate troops. At 31, **Garfield became a brigadier general, two years later a major general of volunteers. Meanwhile, in 1862, Ohioans elected him to Congress**

Ulysses S. Grant 1869-77

Late in the administration of Andrew Johnson, Gen. Ulysses S. Grant quarreled with the President and aligned himself with the Radical Republicans. He was, as the symbol of Union victory during the Civil War, their logical candidate for President in 1868.

When he was elected, the American people hoped for an end to turmoil. Grant provided neither vigor nor reform. Looking to Congress for direction, he seemed bewildered. One visitor to the White House noted "a puzzled pathos, as of a man with a problem before him of which he does not understand the terms."

Born in 1822, Grant was the son of an Ohio tanner. He went to **West Point rather against his will and graduated in the middle of his class. In** the **Mexican War he fought under Gen. Zachary Taylor**.

At the outbreak of the Civil War, Grant was working in his father's leather store in Galena, Illinois. He was appointed by the Governor to command an unruly volunteer regiment. Grant whipped it into shape and by September 1861 he had risen to the rank of brigadier general of volunteers

Warren G. Harding 1921-23

Before his nomination, Warren G. Harding declared, "America's present need is not heroics, but healing; not nostrums, but normalcy; not revolution, but restoration; not agitation, but adjustment; not surgery, but serenity; not the dramatic, but the dispassionate; not experiment, but equipoise; not submergence in internationality, but containment in triumphant nationality…."

A Democratic leader, William Gibbs McAdoo, called Harding's speeches "an army of pompous phrases moving across the landscape in search of an idea." Their very murkiness was effective, since Harding's pronouncements remained unclear on the League of Nations, in contrast to the impassioned crusade of the Democratic candidates, Governor James M. Cox of Ohio and Franklin D. Roosevelt.

Thirty-one distinguished Republicans had signed a manifesto assuring voters that a vote for Harding was a vote for the League. But Harding interpreted his election as a mandate to stay out of the League of Nations.

Harding, born near Marion, Ohio, in 1865, became the publisher of a newspaper. He married a divorcee, Mrs. Florence Kling De Wolfe. **He was a trustee of the Trinity Baptist Church, a director of almost every important business, and a leader in fraternal organizations and charitable enterprises.**

Benjamin Harrison 1889-93

Nominated for President on the eighth ballot at the 1888 Republican Convention, Benjamin Harrison conducted one of the first "front-porch" campaigns, delivering short speeches to delegations that visited him in Indianapolis. As he was only 5 feet, 6 inches tall, Democrats called him "Little Ben"; Republicans replied that he was big enough to wear the hat of his grandfather, "Old Tippecanoe."

Born in 1833 on a farm by the Ohio River below Cincinnati, Harrison **attended Miami University in Ohio and read law in Cincinnati.** He moved to Indianapolis, where he **practiced law** and campaigned for the Republican Party. He married Caroline Lavinia Scott in 1853. **After the Civil War—he was Colonel of the 70th Volunteer Infantry—Harrison became a pillar of Indianapolis, enhancing his reputation as a brilliant lawyer.**

The Democrats defeated him for Governor of Indiana in 1876 by unfairly stigmatizing him as "Kid Gloves" Harrison. In the 1880's he served in the United States Senate, where he championed Indians, homesteaders and Civil War veterans.

William Henry Harrison 1841

"Give him a barrel of hard cider and settle a pension of two thousand a year on him, and my word for it," a Democratic newspaper foolishly gibed, "he will sit ... by the side of a 'sea coal' fire, and study moral philosophy. "The Whigs, seizing on this political misstep, in 1840 presented their candidate William Henry Harrison as a simple frontier Indian fighter, living in a log cabin and drinking cider, in sharp contrast to an aristocratic champagne-sipping Van Buren.

Harrison was in fact a scion of the Virginia planter aristocracy. He was born at Berkeley in 1773. He **studied classics and history at Hampden-Sydney College, and then began the study of medicine in Richmond.**

Suddenly, that same year, 1791, Harrison switched interests. He **obtained a commission as ensign in the First Infantry of the Regular Army,** and headed to the Northwest, where he spent much of his life

In the campaign against the Indians, Harrison served as aide-de-camp to General "Mad Anthony" Wayne at the Battle of Fallen Timbers, which opened most of the Ohio area to settlement. **After resigning from the Army in 1798, he became Secretary of the Northwest Territory, was its first delegate to Congress**, and helped obtain legislation dividing the Territory into the Northwest and Indiana Territories. **In 1801 he became Governor of the Indiana Territory, serving 12 years.**

Rutherford B. Hayes 1877-81

Beneficiary of the most fiercely disputed election in American history, Rutherford B. Hayes brought to the Executive Mansion dignity, honesty, and moderate reform.

To the delight of the Woman's Christian Temperance Union, Lucy Webb Hayes carried out her husband's orders to banish wines and liquors from the White House.

Born in Ohio in 1822, Hayes was **educated at Kenyon College and Harvard Law School. After five years of law practice in Lower Sandusky, he moved to Cincinnati, where he flourished as a young Whig lawyer**

Herbert Hoover 1929-33

Son of a Quaker blacksmith, Herbert Clark Hoover brought to the Presidency an unparalleled reputation for public service as an engineer, administrator, and humanitarian.

Born in an Iowa village in 1874, he grew up in Oregon. He **enrolled at Stanford University when it opened in 1891, graduating as a mining engineer**.

He married his Stanford sweetheart, Lou Henry, and they went to China, where he worked for a private corporation as China's leading engineer. In June 1900 the Boxer Rebellion caught the Hoovers in Tientsin.

For almost a month the settlement was under heavy fire. While his wife worked in the hospitals, Hoover directed the building of barricades, and once risked his life rescuing Chinese children

After capably serving as **Secretary of Commerce under Presidents Harding** and Coolidge, Hoover became the Republican Presidential nominee in 1928. He said then: "We in America today are nearer to the final triumph over poverty than ever before in the history of any land." His election seemed to ensure prosperity. Yet within months the stock market crashed, and the Nation spiraled downward into depression.

Andrew Jackson –1829-37

More nearly than any of his predecessors, Andrew Jackson was elected by popular vote; as President he sought to act as the direct representative of the common man.

Born in a backwoods settlement in the Carolinas in 1767, he **received sporadic education**. But in his late teens he read law for about two years, and he **became an outstanding young lawyer** in Tennessee. Fiercely jealous of his honor, he engaged in brawls, and in a duel killed a man who cast an unjustified slur on his wife Rachel.

Jackson prospered sufficiently to buy slaves and to build a mansion, the Hermitage, near Nashville. **He was the first man elected from Tennessee to the House of Representatives, and he served briefly in the Senate. A major general in the War of 1812,** Jackson became a national hero when he defeated the British at New Orleans.

Thomas Jefferson 1801-09

In the thick of party conflict in 1800, Thomas Jefferson wrote in a private letter, "I have sworn upon the altar of God eternal hostility against every form of tyranny over the mind of man."

This powerful advocate of liberty was born in 1743 in Albermarle County, Virginia, **inheriting from his father, a planter and surveyor**, some 5,000 acres of land, and from his mother, a Randolph, high social standing. **He studied at the College of William and Mary, and then read law.** In 1772 he married Martha Wayles Skelton, a widow, and took her to live in his partly constructed mountaintop home, Monticello

Andrew Johnson 1865-69

With the Assassination of Lincoln, the Presidency fell upon an old-fashioned southern Jacksonian Democrat of pronounced states' rights views. Although an honest and honorable man, Andrew Johnson was **one of the most unfortunate of Presidents.** Arrayed against him were the Radical Republicans in Congress, brilliantly led and ruthless in their tactics. Johnson was no match for them.

Born in Raleigh, North Carolina, in 1808, **Johnson grew up in poverty. He was apprenticed to a tailor as a boy, but ran away. He opened a tailor shop in Greeneville, Tennessee,** married Eliza McCardle, and **participated in debates at the local academy.**

Entering politics, he became an adept stump speaker, championing the common man and vilifying the plantation aristocracy. As **a Member of the House of Representatives and the Senate in the 1840's and '50's,** he advocated a homestead bill to provide a free farm for the poor man.

Lyndon B. Johnson 1963-69

"A Great Society" for the American people and their fellow men elsewhere was the vision of Lyndon B. Johnson. In his first years of office he obtained passage of one of the most extensive legislative programs in the Nation's history. Maintaining collective security, he carried on the rapidly growing struggle to restrain Communist encroachment in Viet Nam.

Johnson was born on August 27, 1908, in central Texas, not far from Johnson City, which his family had helped settle. He felt the pinch of rural poverty as he grew up, **working his way through Southwest Texas State Teachers College;** he learned compassion for the poverty of others when he **taught students of Mexican descent.**

In 1937 he **campaigned successfully for the House of Representatives** on a New Deal platform, effectively aided by his wife, the former Claudia "Lady Bird" Taylor, whom he had married in 1934.

During World War II he **served briefly in the Navy as a lieutenant commander, winning a Silver Star in the South Pacific.** After **six terms**

in the House, Johnson was **elected to the Senate in 1948**. In **1953, he became the youngest Minority Leader in Senate history**, and the following year, when the Democrats won control, Majority Leader. With rare skill he obtained passage of a number of key Eisenhower measures.

In the 1960 campaign, **Johnson, as John F. Kennedy's running mate, was elected Vice President.** On November 22, 1963, when Kennedy was assassinated, Johnson was sworn in as President

John Kennedy 1961-63

On November 22, 1963, when he was hardly past his first thousand days in office, John Fitzgerald Kennedy was killed by an assassin's bullets as his motorcade wound through Dallas, Texas. Kennedy was the youngest man elected President; he was the youngest to die.

Of Irish descent, he was born in Brookline, Massachusetts, on May 29, 1917. **Graduating from Harvard in 1940, he entered the Navy. In 1943**, when his PT boat was rammed and sunk by a Japanese destroyer, Kennedy, despite grave injuries, led the survivors through perilous waters to safety.

Back from the war, he became a Democratic **Congressman** from the Boston area, **advancing in 1953 to the Senate.** He married Jacqueline Bouvier on September 12, 1953. In 1955, while recuperating from a back operation, he **wrote** Profiles in Courage, **which won the Pulitzer Prize in history**.

In 1956 Kennedy almost gained the Democratic nomination for Vice President, and four years later was a first-ballot nominee for President. Millions watched his television debates with the Republican candidate, Richard M. Nixon. Winning by a narrow margin in the popular vote, Kennedy became the first Roman Catholic President.

Abraham Lincoln 1861-65

Lincoln warned the South in his Inaugural Address: "In your hands, my dissatisfied fellow countrymen, and not in mine, is the momentous issue of civil war. The government will not assail you…. You have no oath registered in Heaven to destroy the government, while I shall have the most solemn one to preserve, protect and defend it."

Lincoln thought secession illegal, and was willing to use force to defend Federal law and the Union. When confederate batteries fired on Fort Sumter and forced its surrender, he called on the states for 75,000 volunteers. Four more slave states joined the Confederacy but four remained within the Union. The Civil War had begun.

The son of a Kentucky frontiersman, **Lincoln had to struggle for a living and for learning.** Five months before receiving his party's nomination for President, he sketched his life:

Lincoln made extraordinary efforts to attain knowledge while working on a farm, splitting rails for fences, and keeping store at New Salem, Illinois. **He was a captain in the Black Hawk War, spent eight**

years in the Illinois legislature, and rode the circuit of courts for many years. **His law partner said of him, "His ambition was a little engine that knew no rest."**

James Madison 1809-17

At his inauguration, James Madison, a small, wizened man, appeared old and worn; Washington Irving described him as "but a withered little apple-John." But whatever his deficiencies in charm, Madison's buxom wife Dolley compensated for them with her warmth and gaiety. She was the toast of Washington.

Born in 1751, Madison was brought up in Orange County, Virginia, and **attended Princeton (then called the College of New Jersey). A student of history and government, well-read in law,** he **participated in the framing of the Virginia Constitution in 1776, served in the Continental Congress, and was a leader in the Virginia Assembly.**

When delegates to the Constitutional Convention assembled at Philadelphia, the 36-year-old Madison took frequent and emphatic part in the debates.

Madison made a major contribution to the ratification of the Constitution by writing, with Alexander Hamilton and John Jay, the *Federalist* essays. In later years, when he was referred to as the "Father of the Constitution," Madison protested that the document was not "the off-spring of a single brain," but "the work of many heads and many hands."

In Congress, he helped frame the Bill of Rights and enact the first revenue legislation.

William McKinley 1897-1901

At the 1896 Republican Convention, in time of depression, the wealthy Cleveland businessman Marcus Alonzo Hanna ensured the nomination of his friend William McKinley as "the advance agent of prosperity." The Democrats, advocating the "free and unlimited coinage of both silver and gold"—which would have mildly inflated the currency—nominated William Jennings Bryan.

While Hanna used large contributions from eastern Republicans frightened by Bryan's views on silver, McKinley met delegations on his front porch in Canton, Ohio. He won by the largest majority of popular votes since 1872.

Born in Niles, Ohio, in 1843, McKinley briefly **attended Allegheny College**, and was **teaching in a country school** when the Civil War broke out. Enlisting as **a private in the Union Army**, he was mustered out at the end of the war as a brevet major of volunteers. **He studied law, opened an office in Canton, Ohio,** and married Ida Saxton, daughter of a local banker.

At 34, McKinley **won a seat in Congress**. His attractive personality, exemplary character, and quick intelligence enabled him to rise rapidly. He was appointed to the powerful Ways and Means Committee. Robert M. La

Follette, Sr., who served with him, recalled that he generally "represented the newer view," and "on the great new questions was generally on the side of the public and against private interests."

During his 14 years in the House, he became the leading Republican tariff expert, giving his name to the measure enacted in 1890. The next year he was elected Governor of Ohio, serving two terms.

James Monroe 1817-25

On New Year's Day, 1825, at the last of his annual White House receptions, President James Monroe made a pleasing impression upon a Virginia lady who shook his hand:

"He is tall and well formed. His dress plain and in the old style…. His manner was quiet and dignified. From the frank, honest expression of his eye … I think he well deserves the encomium passed upon him by the great Jefferson, who said, 'Monroe was so honest that if you turned his soul inside out there would not be a spot on it.' "

Born in Westmoreland County, Virginia, in 1758, Monroe **attended the College of William and Mary, fought with distinction in the Continental Army, and practiced law in Fredericksburg, Virginia.**

As a youthful politician, he joined the anti-Federalists in the Virginia Convention which ratified the Constitution, and in 1790, an advocate of Jeffersonian policies, was **elected United States Senator. As Minister**

to France in 1794-1796, he displayed strong sympathies for the French cause; later, with Robert R. Livingston, he helped negotiate the Louisiana Purchase.

Richard M. Nixon 1969-74

Reconciliation was the first goal set by President Richard M. Nixon. The Nation was painfully divided, with turbulence in the cities and war overseas. During his Presidency, Nixon succeeded in ending American fighting in Viet Nam and improving relations with the U.S.S.R. and China. But the Watergate scandal brought fresh divisions to the country and ultimately led to his resignation.

His election in 1968 had climaxed a career unusual on two counts: his early success and his comeback after being defeated for President in 1960 and for Governor of California in 1962.

Born in California in 1913, Nixon had a brilliant record at **Whittier College** and **Duke University Law School** before beginning the practice of law. In 1940, he married Patricia Ryan; they had two daughters, Patricia (Tricia) and Julie. During World War II, **Nixon served as a Navy lieutenant commander in the Pacific.**

On leaving the service, he was **elected to Congress** from his California district. In 1950, **he won a Senate seat.** Two years later, **General Eisenhower selected Nixon, age 39, to be his running mate.**

As Vice President, Nixon took on major duties in the Eisenhower Administration.

Franklin Pierce 1853-57

Franklin Pierce became President at a time of apparent tranquility. The United States, by virtue of the Compromise of 1850, seemed to have weathered its sectional storm. By pursuing the recommendations of southern advisers, Pierce—a New Englander—hoped to prevent still another outbreak of that storm. But his policies, far from preserving calm, hastened the disruption of the Union.

Born in Hillsborough, New Hampshire, in 1804, Pierce **attended Bowdoin College. After graduation he studied law, and then entered politics**. At 24 he was elected to the **New Hampshire legislature; two years later he became its Speaker.** During the 1830's he went to Washington, first as a Representative, then as a Senator.

Pierce, after serving in the Mexican War, was proposed by New Hampshire friends for the Presidential nomination in 1852. At the Democratic Convention, the delegates agreed easily enough upon a platform pledging undeviating support of the Compromise of 1850 and hostility to any efforts to agitate the slavery question. But they balloted 48 times and eliminated all the well-known candidates before nominating Pierce, a true "dark horse."

James K. Polk 1845-49

Often referred to as the first "dark horse" President, James K. Polk was the last of the Jacksonians to sit in the White House, and the last strong President until the Civil War.

He was born in Mecklenburg County, North Carolina, in **1795. Studious and industrious, Polk was graduated with honors in 1818 from the University of North Carolina.** As a young **lawyer** he entered politics, **served in the Tennessee legislature,** and became a friend of Andrew Jackson.

In the House of Representatives, Polk was a chief lieutenant of Jackson in his Bank war. He served as Speaker between 1835 and 1839, leaving to become Governor of Tennessee.

Ronald Reagan 1981-89

At the end of his two terms in office, Ronald Reagan viewed with satisfaction the achievements of his innovative program known as the Reagan Revolution, which aimed to reinvigorate the American people and reduce their reliance upon Government. He felt he had fulfilled his campaign pledge of 1980 to restore "the great, confident roar of American progress and growth and optimism."

On February 6, 1911, Ronald Wilson Reagan was born to Nelle and John Reagan in Tampico, Illinois. **He attended high school in nearby**

Dixon and then worked his way through Eureka College. There, he **studied economics and sociology**, played on the football team, and acted in school plays. **Upon graduation, he became a radio sports announcer. Screen tests in 1937 won him a contract in Hollywood. During the next two decades he appeared in 53 films.**

From his first marriage to actress Jane Wyman, he had two children, Maureen and Michael. Maureen passed away in 2001. In 1952 he married Nancy Davis, who was also an actress, and they had two children, Patricia Ann and Ronald Prescott.

As **president of the Screen Actors Guild**, Reagan became embroiled in disputes over the issue of Communism in the film industry; his political views shifted from liberal to conservative. He toured the country as a television host, becoming a spokesman for conservatism. In 1966 he was elected Governor of California by a margin of a million votes; he was re-elected in 1970.

Franklin D. Roosevelt 1933-45

Assuming the Presidency at the depth of the Great Depression, Franklin D. Roosevelt helped the American people regain faith in them. He brought hope as he promised prompt, vigorous action, and asserted in his Inaugural Address, "the only thing we have to fear is fear itself."

Born in 1882 at Hyde Park, New York—now a national historic site—he **attended Harvard University and Columbia Law School.** On St.

Patrick's Day, 1905, he married Eleanor Roosevelt.

Following the example of his fifth cousin, President Theodore Roosevelt, whom he greatly admired, Franklin D. Roosevelt entered public service through politics, but as a Democrat. He won election to the New York Senate in 1910. **President Wilson appointed him Assistant Secretary of the Navy, and he was the Democratic nominee for Vice President in 1920.**

In the summer of 1921, when he was 39, disaster hit-he was stricken with poliomyelitis. Demonstrating indomitable courage, he fought to regain the use of his legs, particularly through swimming. At the 1924 Democratic Convention he dramatically appeared on crutches to nominate Alfred E. Smith as "the Happy Warrior." **In 1928 Roosevelt became Governor of New York.**

Theodore Roosevelt 1901-09

With the assassination of President McKinley, Theodore Roosevelt, not quite 43, became the youngest President in the Nation's history. He brought new excitement and power to the Presidency, as he vigorously led Congress and the American public toward progressive reforms and a strong foreign policy.

He took the view that the President as a "steward of the people" should take whatever action necessary for the public good unless expressly forbidden by law or the Constitution." I did not usurp power," he wrote, "but I did greatly broaden the use of executive power."

Roosevelt's youth differed sharply from that of the log cabin Presidents. **He was born in New York City in 1858 into a wealthy family**, but he too struggled—against ill health—and in his triumph became an advocate of the strenuous life.

During the Spanish-American War, **Roosevelt was Lieutenant Colonel of the Rough Rider Regiment,** which he led on a charge at the battle of San Juan. **He was one of the most conspicuous heroes of the war.**

William Howard Taft 1909-13

Distinguished jurist, effective administrator, but poor politician, William Howard Taft spent four uncomfortable years in the White House. Large, jovial, conscientious, he was caught in the intense battles between Progressives and conservatives, and got scant credit for the achievements of his administration.

Born in 1857, the son of a distinguished judge, he was **graduated from Yale, and returned to Cincinnati to study and practice law**. He rose in politics through Republican judiciary appointments, through his own competence and availability, and because, as he once wrote facetiously, he always had his "plate the right side up when offices were falling."

But Taft much preferred law to politics. **He was appointed a Federal circuit judge at 34.** He aspired to be a member of the Supreme Court, but his wife, Helen Herron Taft, held other ambitions for him.

Zachary Taylor 1849-50

Northerners and Southerners disputed sharply whether the territories wrested from Mexico should be opened to slavery, and some Southerners even threatened secession. Standing firm, Zachary Taylor was prepared to hold the Union together by armed force rather than by compromise.

Born in Virginia in 1784, he was taken as an infant to Kentucky and raised on a plantation. He was a **career officer in the Army**, but his talk was most often of cotton raising. His home was in Baton Rouge, Louisiana, and he owned a plantation in Mississippi. But Taylor did not defend slavery or southern sectionalism; **40 years in the Army made him a strong nationalist.**

Harry S. Truman 1945-53

During his few weeks as Vice President, Harry S. Truman scarcely saw President Roosevelt, and received no briefing on the development of the atomic bomb or the unfolding difficulties with Soviet Russia. Suddenly these and a host of other wartime problems became Truman's to solve when, on April 12, 1945, he became President. He told reporters, "I felt like the moon, the stars, and all the planets had fallen on me."

Truman was born in Lamar, Missouri, in 1884. He grew up in Independence, and for **12 years prospered as a Missouri farmer.**

He went to France during World War I as a captain in the Field Artillery. Returning, he married Elizabeth Virginia Wallace, and opened a haberdashery in Kansas City.

Active in the Democratic Party, Truman was **elected a judge of the Jackson County Court (an administrative position) in 1922. He became a Senator in 1934. During World War II he headed the Senate war investigating committee, checking into waste and corruption and saving perhaps as much as 15 billion dollars.**

John Tyler 1841-45

Dubbed "His Accidence" by his detractors, John Tyler was the first Vice President to be elevated to the office of President by the death of his predecessor.

Born in Virginia in 1790, he was raised believing that the Constitution must be strictly construed. He never wavered from this conviction. He attended the College of William and Mary and **studied law**.

Serving in the House of Representatives from 1816 to 1821, Tyler voted against most nationalist legislation and opposed the Missouri Compromise. After leaving the House he **served twice as Governor of Virginia**. As **a Senator** he reluctantly supported Jackson for President as a choice of evils. Tyler soon joined the states' rights Southerners in Congress who banded with Henry Clay, Daniel Webster, and their newly formed Whig party opposing President Jackson

The Whigs nominated Tyler for Vice President in 1840, hoping for support from southern states'-righters who could not stomach Jacksonian Democracy. The slogan "Tippecanoe and Tyler Too" implied flagwaving nationalism plus a dash of southern sectionalism.

Martin Van Buren 1837-41

Only about 5 feet, 6 inches tall, but trim and erect, Martin Van Buren dressed fastidiously. His impeccable appearance belied his amiability—and his humble background. Of Dutch descent, he was born in 1782, the son of a tavern keeper and farmer, in Kinderhook, New York.

As **a** young **lawyer** he became involved in New York politics. As leader of the "Albany Regency," an effective New York political organization, he shrewdly dispensed public offices and bounty in a fashion calculated to bring votes. Yet he faithfully fulfilled official duties, and in **1821 was elected to the United States Senate.**

By 1827 he had emerged as the principal northern leader for Andrew Jackson. President Jackson rewarded Van Buren by **appointing him Secretary of State**. As the Cabinet Members appointed at John C. Calhoun's recommendation began to demonstrate only secondary loyalty to Jackson, Van Buren emerged as the President's most trusted adviser. Jackson referred to him as, "a true man with no guile."

George Washington 1789-97

On April 30, 1789, George Washington, standing on the balcony of Federal Hall on Wall Street in New York, took his oath of office as the first President of the United States. "As the first of every thing, in our situation will serve to establish a Precedent," he wrote James Madison, "it is devoutly wished on my part, that these precedents may be fixed on true principles."

Born in 1732 into a Virginia planter family, **he learned the morals, manners, and body of knowledge requisite for an 18th century Virginia gentleman.**

He pursued two intertwined interests: military arts and western expansion. At 16 he helped survey Shenandoah lands for Thomas, Lord Fairfax. Commissioned a lieutenant colonel in 1754, he fought the first skirmishes of what grew into the French and Indian War. The next year, as an aide to Gen. Edward Braddock, he escaped injury although four bullets ripped his coat and two horses were shot from under him.

When the Second Continental Congress assembled in Philadelphia in May 1775, Washington, one of the Virginia delegates, was elected Commander in Chief of the Continental Army. On July 3, 1775, at Cambridge, Massachusetts, he took command of his ill-trained troops and embarked upon a war that was to last six grueling years.

Paula Diane Harris
Woodrow Wilson 1913-21

Like Roosevelt before him, Woodrow Wilson regarded himself as the personal representative of the people. "No one but the President," he said, "seems to be expected ... to look out for the general interests of the country." He developed a program of progressive reform and asserted international leadership in building a new world order. In 1917 he proclaimed American entrance into World War I a crusade to make the world "safe for democracy."

Wilson had seen the frightfulness of war. He was born in Virginia in 1856, the son of a Presbyterian minister who during the Civil War was a pastor in Augusta, Georgia, and during Reconstruction a professor in the charred city of Columbia, South Carolina.

After graduation from Princeton (then the College of New Jersey) and the University of Virginia Law School, Wilson earned his doctorate at Johns Hopkins University and entered upon an academic career. In 1885 he married Ellen Louise Axson.

Wilson advanced rapidly as a conservative **young professor of political science** and became president of Princeton in 1902. His growing national reputation led some conservative Democrats to consider him Presidential timber. First they **persuaded him to run for Governor of New Jersey in 1910**. In the campaign he asserted his independence of the conservatives and of the machine that had nominated him, endorsing a progressive platform, which he pursued as governor.

Footnote: White House Historical Association with cooperation

National Geographic Society

Obtaining a Major Political Party Nomination

The American system for nominating the candidates for president of the United States is complex and confused. Ever since the 1970s when the Democrat and Republican parties began to reform the rules for selecting their presidential and vice presidential nominees, the system has been in a state of turbulence, with the most successful candidates being those who understand its complexities, able to mobilize funds and able to maneuver within and around them. But after all, that is what creative politicians do — master the game of politics and play hardball with the skill to defeat their opponents. Importantly, a candidate for the presidency must be creative in obtaining funding for its candidacy. Howard Dean, former presidential candidate for the 2004 presidency was creative in raising the bar to use the internet to raise millions of dollars for his campaign.

Money matters as we approach yet another presidential election in which the vote seems too close to call. What will determine the outcome of the 2004 presidential election? Money! The average citizen thinks that it will be the best ideas and best organization that will win. They will play a part but campaign 2004 financial capital will be a key factor.

Remember, we get one vote on November 2nd to have our democracy voices heard. But money obtains vote's everyday. Each time you turn on the radio or television money is getting votes. Each time a candidate hands out literature about their ideas, money is there to obtain votes. Every time you read the newspapers, listen to the radio or television, money is there to obtain votes. Each time you go out on the internet money is there to obtain votes. Every time the airplane, bus, car, train carries the candidate to your community; money is there to obtain votes.

It is important to do your own research on the candidates so that when you get to the polls you understand what you are voting for. No longer can voters go strictly by the media, who tries to choose the winner before the election, persuading voters depending on which candidate gives them the most money. Also remember, these media sources are probably owned by either a Democrat or a Republican. The spin they place on the news that comes into your home is already tainted in many instances to give you the information they want you to have not necessarily the true and complete picture. John Kerry for instance is running on his three purple hearts from the Vietnam War and his silver and bronze medals when he served in Vietnam for only about four months. The American people need to hear his voting record in the Senate! Kerry has no problem with pointing out Bush's record why doesn't he run on his own political record? Do your homework prior to voting. Remember that in the general election you do not have to vote on straight party lines. In other words, you are able to vote for a Republican, Democrat and or even an independent candidate or another party affiliation. Be loyal to the issues and to how the candidate stands on those issues that affect you and not be loyal to a particular party. Be concerned in voting for incumbents that do not stand on their political records who run their elections on everything but their records.

Voters also must be aware that campaign contributions to political candidates are seen as investments designed to yield a return and influence. Money *does* come with strings attached. Do your research, which is public information, finding out who is financing the candidates campaign. Special interests who finance the candidates campaign own the candidate. The candidate has already been sold and after election becomes just a figurehead taking direction from those that financed their campaigns. Every candidate has to sell something in order to be elected because you need money, just make sure you know what you are giving up prior to taking the funds. I'm not talking about ten dollars here and a hundred dollars there, or even a few thousand. I'm talking about double or triple thousands from one source. Clearly understand what it is they want from you if you should be elected.

The role big money plays in politics also undermines democracy. Any democracy is based on the concept of "one person, one vote." But the overwhelming role money plays in American politics creates something called the "weighted vote." Sarah gives her vote plus $100 to candidate A; Sam gives his vote and $1,000 to candidate B. whose vote has more clout? When wealthy individuals and large corporation's donate large sums of money to politics it creates legalized corruption: technically legal, but definitely corrupt.

The amount of money we are talking about is over 100 million dollars for each Kerry and Bush campaigns for president. Let's face it the average black couldn't raise that level of financial resources against a white candidate for president. If every Black American in this country would donate $1.00 to a qualified black candidate the possibilities would be endless. Black's unfortunately and with valid cause havn't been able to trust each other as a race enough to support one another and whites know it and therefore don't consider us a competition. Black Americans do well as individuals but as a group we rate an F.

Civil Rights organizations don't support black presidential candidates because they don't think they can win and they need a "sugar daddy" to keep those contributions coming into their organizations. Contributions from Democrats and Republicans and anything or anyone else that sends theses organizations money is an accepted membership of the organization. The leaderships of these non-profit organizations realize the importance in continuing to receive donations that will enable them to keep those hefty salaries and fringe benefits. Civil Rights on the national level have become a large lucrative business.

On the other side of the coin don't depend on the black church to raise the money for your campaign. Many are busy trying to appeal to those in the church that pay their tithes. Churches today instead of saving souls and nurturing the family many of them are applying for local, state and federal contracts for their independent church projects keeping up with other church memberships. Today, being a minister has become an occupation with fat salaries and fringe benefits such as homes, cars, and vacations. The calling from God to preach the gospel has been replaced with the calling for tithes. The Ten Commandments in how we should live and treat each other have become the commandments of "Thou shall give the minister".

Black Americans are the most praying folk I've ever met. Always kissing, hugging each other as they greet you in church. Preaching great sermons singing praises that make you cry. But right after the service the way we treat each other, the way we wag our tongues and how we don't support one another, and sell each other out for the dollar menu at McDonalds is keeping us at the back of the bus. The KKK doesn't have to worry about destroying blacks in America because we are doing a good job ourselves.

I've told you what you need regarding money and I've told you where you won't get it! To put it simpler, money in this world, grace in the next. In order for a black to be taken serious as a candidate for the presidency they will have to be skilled in raising capitol for their campaign which means they must be able to appeal to all cultures and the biggest culture is white males.

In order to better understand the process you need to understand the history. Political Science and Public Administration courses need to be offered on a high school level as an elective in public schools. This will prepare students those who are interested in public service careers of the requirements and qualifications of public servant positions. This may eliminate politicians who master the skill to defeat their opponents but who are not qualified once they are in office.

Have you ever met a person who beat their opponent but turned out they weren't qualified to serve in the position? Have you ever witnessed a promotion and wondered how that person got it because they weren't qualified? When we look at TV show examples such as:

- Big Brother
- Survivor
- Bachelor
- Extreme Makeover

...does America realize we are teaching our young people how to beat someone out of something instead of earning it the old fashioned way through education and or technical skill and good old fashion hard work? Through these types of shows we are teaching our young people how to be superficial and not real. We are teaching our children they are not born good enough that by age 12 they need a makeover. These are superficial behaviors. Each parent unknowingly could be raising the next black president of the Untied States. At risk children are big business. Think about it and more important think about who is helping them to become "at risk"?

Another area of concern is getting career politicians to run on their voting record. It is becoming more and more difficult; in fact they run their campaigns on everything but their voting records. In order for voters to be able to choose a candidate who reflects their issues they need to know the candidates voting record and as much about the candidate's professional experience as possible.

Have you ever heard a candidate make a statement that their opponent's ideas won't work but they never, ever tell you what they will do to make it better and how they will accomplish the task? If a candidate can't think on their feet, give intelligent ideas and communicate effectively how they will accomplish their thoughts then how can they possibly succeed in fulfilling their promise?

If you run for the presidency or any elected office run on your voting record if you are an incumbent as well as your education and experience. It will show voters even if they disagree on your position that you stand firm in your beliefs. Be prepared to debate why you believe in the issues as you do. Don't flip flop over issues and your record and don't be afraid to admit a mistake. People learn from their mistakes not from their successes. Appeal to the human side of voters and be firm in your beliefs.

As a Black candidate you have other obstacles to overcome such as financial resources and the fact that you are a black candidate therefore you must appeal to the white voter. Like the white candidate who courts the black vote you must be able to cross cultures and court all voters. It is achievable but it will take style, grace, education, political experience, constructive criticism, wit and creativity to succeed, NOT the ghetto style or ghetto speech. Even with the educational accomplishments to be accepted as a serious candidate you must have a style that will cross cultures. Remember, for the presidency you are not running in just black communities. The entire country votes for you therefore, your issues and demeanor must appeal to all cultures.

As we saw in the 2004 democrat primaries across the nation, the process of how we select a political nominee needs to be changed. There should be one primary across the nation for voters to choose their party's nominee. Iowa, the first state, New Hampshire second, during the primary it seemed as though the rest of the states followed suit with the help of the media in choosing the Democrat nominee. One or two states out of 52 should not choose a political party's nominee or the president of the United States and neither should the media. This is not democracy. In addition, neither major political party, Republican or Democrat, are parties of the people. Both parties have failed in this aspect when their priority is corporate America and the special interests, not the people.

Blacks unfortunately in this country have little corporate ownership. This would help the black presidential candidate to gain equal financial support from corporate America against a white contender. A black candidate will get donations but in no way will it come close to the financial contributions a white candidate can obtain. Money alone will break a campaign. This is why it is becoming more and more important that Blacks begin to build up their economic base developing more business ownership to enable them to increase their economic power. Once that has been accomplished the next step is to work on getting blacks to feel comfortable investing in each other.

When blacks invest the "black dollar" back in themselves the resulting economic growth will increase their fiscal and political power in this country.

Evolution of Parties and Primaries

A reason the nomination process keeps changing is that, unlike the system of electing the president, it is not enumerated in the U.S.

Constitution. It also was not a calculated omission by those who drafted the constitutional design. The absence of a procedure for party nomination stems from no political parties in existence at the time the Constitution was formulated and ratified. Political parties developed after the government began to function and in response to the policies of the first administration, that of President George Washington

Were you aware that beginning in 1796, members of Congress who identified with one of the political parties of the time met informally to decide on their party's presidential and vice presidential nominees? Known as "King Caucus," this system for selecting party candidates continued for almost 30 years. It failed in 1828, a victim of changes in the partisan composition of the electorate that permitted one party, the Democratic-Republicans, to emerge and become the only viable national party. In the absence of two-party competition, factions developed within the Democratic-Republican Party, making it impossible for its congressional representatives to agree on a consensus candidate.

King Caucus was replaced by National nominating conventions. In 1831 a small minor party, the Anti-Masons, met in a tavern to select its presidential and vice presidential candidates and a platform on which they would run. Since then, the major parties and many minor parties have held national nominating conventions, attended by delegates from the states, to choose presidential and vice presidential nominees, agreeing on their policy positions to represent their views.

During the 19th century and into the 20th the conventions were controlled by state party leaders who chose the delegates, they also influenced their voting behavior at these national meetings. This still occurs today. The power of the party leaders and the tight-fisted way in which they exercised it became a political issue. Those who disliked having unshakable party bosses handpick the presidential nominees decided to support democratic reforms. States began to enact laws that permitted primary elections in which rank-and-file partisans were able to indicate their preferences. By 1916 more than half of the states held some kind of primary election.

The lobby group to encourage more people to participate in their party's selection process was short-lived. Subsequently at the end of World War I, party leaders, who saw these elections as a threat to their own influence, persuaded state legislatures to abolish them on the grounds that they were expensive, they did not attract many voters, and some major candidates refused to run in them. Moreover, the primaries frequently encouraged conflict within the parties, thereby weakening their organizational structure and making them less capable of competing in the general election. By 1936, only about a dozen states continued to hold presidential primaries.

Democratic pressures reemerged following World War II. Additionally, the arrival of television provided a communications medium through which people could see and hear the campaign in their own living rooms. Television also gave the candidates a forum to demonstrate their popularity and delectability. Dwight Eisenhower, John Kennedy, and Richard Nixon all entered the primaries to prove to their party that a general, a Catholic, and a once-defeated presidential candidate could win in the general election. And they did.

Indirectly, the Vietnam War and the divisions it engendered within the United States also created pressure to allow the people to choose their party's candidates. The catalyst was the 1968 Democratic Party nominating process and events that surrounded it: the antiwar movement within the party led by Senator Eugene McCarthy, the campaign and assassination of Senator Robert Kennedy, the violent demonstrations that occurred in the streets around the Democratic convention as it was meeting, and the nomination of Vice President Hubert Humphrey who had chosen not to enter the primaries.

In an attempt to try to unify a divided party for its presidential campaign, the delegates at the 1968 Democratic convention agreed to appoint a committee to reexamine the party's presidential nomination process with the twin goals of encouraging greater public participation and improving the representative character of those who attended the convention. Thus began the process by which both major political parties have reformed the way they go about selecting their presidential and vice presidential nominees.

The Primary and Caucus System Today

The major changes that the Democrats instituted have encouraged states (which make election laws for their residents) to hold primary elections. A primary is an election among supporters of the same party to choose that party's candidates who run in the general election. Depending on the laws of the state, voters may cast ballots directly for the presidential candidates themselves or indirectly for delegates who are pledged to support particular candidates. Much is being discussed as some states have adopted to allow open primaries where an independent registered voter can also vote for the candidate of their choice.

The other option that states have under the current system is to hold a multi-staged caucus/convention process in which partisans that live within a relatively small geographic area, a local electoral precinct, get together and select delegates who are pledged to specific candidates. These delegates in turn represent their precinct at a county convention, which chooses delegates to attend the state convention, which selects the delegates to represent the state at the national party conventions. Although this multi-staged caucus/convention system takes several months, the candidate preferences are essentially determined by the voting in the first-round caucus.

The actual size of the state's delegation to the national party convention is calculated on the basis of a formula established by the party that includes considerations of the state's population, its past support for that party's national candidates, and the number of elected officials and party leaders currently serving in office. The allocation formula that the Democrats use results in national conventions that have about twice as many delegates as the Republicans' conventions.

The U.S. Constitution gives the states the authority to make their own election laws, the states are free to establish their own primaries and caucuses and determine the dates on which they will be held. The states have an incentive to conduct primaries and caucuses in accordance with party rules because the U.S. Supreme Court has determined that the parties have a right to prescribe and enforce rules for those attending their nominating conventions. Thus states that select delegates in a manner that does not accord with party rules could find their delegates challenged at the national conventions or the size of their delegations reduced by the party for violating its rules. Today, about 80 percent of the delegates who attend their parties' national nominating conventions are chosen in primary elections that are open to all registered or self-identified Republicans and Democrats.

The Democratic Party has imposed a set of national rules on all its state affiliates; the Republican Party has not. The Democratic rules require states to hold their nomination contest between the first Tuesday of March and the second Tuesday in June during the year in which the general election is held. The small states of Iowa and New Hampshire are given official exemptions to vote earlier because of their tradition of holding the first caucus and the first primary election. The Democrats also require that 75 percent of a state's delegates be elected in districts that are no larger than a congressional district in order to enhance the representation of minorities that may be concentrated in communities within the state. Moreover, the numbers of delegates who are pledged to support specific candidates are selected only in proportion to the vote they or their candidates receive, provided that votes are at least 15 percent of the total. Finally, the Democrats require that state delegations be equally divided between men and women.

The Republicans do not mandate national rules on their state parties. Republican caucuses or primaries can occur at any time, even in the year before the election; states can permit winner-take-all voting in Republican primaries if they choose to do so; Republican candidates do not need to obtain a minimum percentage of the vote in order to gain delegates pledged to them. Republican state delegations do not need to be divided evenly between men and women, although states are encouraged to try to achieve equal gender representation and the broadest possible participation of rank-and-file partisans.

Despite the differences in national rules, two important trends have emerged in both parties in recent elections.

1. More and more states have moved their primaries and caucuses toward the beginning of the process. This keeps them in order to exercise more influence over the selection of the nominee, to encourage the candidates to address the needs and interests of the state, and to get their campaigns to spend money in them. This is known as "front-loading."
2. In a practice known as "regionalization," states have cooperated with others in their regions to hold their primaries and caucuses on the same date to maximize the impact of their region.

Both of these trends have served to compact the process. Candidates due to the system is forced to begin their campaigns earlier concentrating their efforts in the early states. It forces them to raise and spend more money earlier, and to depend increasingly on mass media, particularly radio and television. In addition, they know they need the endorsements of state party leaders to help them reach voters in many states that are conducting their elections on the same day.

The front-loading and regionalization of the nomination process has benefited nationally recognized candidates, as incumbent vice presidents, large-state governors, and U.S. senators, who have access to more money, more media, and more organizational support. These advantages allow front-runners to wage campaigns in several states simultaneously, whereas lesser-known candidates first concentrate their resources and efforts in the early, small-state caucuses and primaries in order to gain the visibility that will allow them to compete with their better-known rivals. The short time frame works against the ability of those who wish to use the early contests as a stepping-stone to the nomination, as a relatively unknown Georgia governor, Jimmy Carter, did in 1976.

Party Nominations and Democracy

In theory, the reforms in the presidential nomination process have enlarged the base of public participation, forced the candidates to make broad-based partisan appeals, and encouraged them, if elected, to stay more in touch with those who have nominated them rather than take their reelection for granted. No longer are presidential candidates beholden to a small group of party leaders who have chosen them and expect something in return. The delegates selected to attend their parties' nominating conventions have become more representative of the demographic groups of voters who have chosen them. These consequences have contributed to the democratization of the presidential nominating process.

On the other hand, even though a larger proportion of the population participates in the nomination process than in the pre-reform period, the participants themselves are still not representative of rank-and-file partisans, much less the general electorate. They are better educated, have higher incomes, and are older than the average Republican or Democratic voter. And the convention delegates they select tend to be more ideologically oriented than their rank-and-file, with Republican delegates more conservative and Democratic delegates more liberal. Moreover, the nomination process has, at times, exacerbated divisions within a party, and the more divisive the process, the more it hurts rather than helps that party and its nominees in the general election.

The current way primaries and caucuses determine the winner has led to anticlimactic nominating conventions as well since the likely nominees are known months before the conventions meet. As a consequence, the parties have turned the conventions into huge pep rallies to launch their presidential campaigns; the press has tried to find news in them, emphasizing conflicts over policy and personal issues; and public interest in the conventions has declined. In recent years convention news coverage is down, and television viewer ship has fallen off. Yet for many Americans the conventions are still a major event on the road to choosing a president[1].

As you can see running for the presidency takes more then just standing at a podium and announcing your candidacy. If you do not know how the system works then you will need to hire someone who does and take his or her direction for your campaign. We have reviewed the qualifications and requirements to become the President of the United States. In addition, we have reviewed the education and experience from each of the past elected presidents. Notice their education and levels of accomplishments. Notice their experience in previous political positions that range from government appointments to elected congress to senate positions and military leadership.

It is important that if you cannot master the art of politics how to play hard and skillfully you will not be successful in American politics. The only other option is to completely sell yourself to special interests that have the money to fund your campaign. I briefly touched on this subject earlier. The problem with this is they will own your position on issues after the election and strip you of your ideas and integrity. This is not the route you want to take. Politicians are no good to themselves or their constituents if they place themselves in bondage to the higher bidder. Many politicians follow this avenue in order to fund their campaigns. Black businesses, churches and communities need to band together to help fund black candidate campaigns helping to eliminate candidates placing themselves in bondage to special interests. There are different forms of prostitution and all forms should be avoided. You get nothing for nothing there is always a cost involved and the charge is not always money.

Paula Diane Harris

Black American Economic Crunch

Blacks did earn 64 cents for every dollar earned by Whites, up from 59 cents ten years ago. Not only was Black unemployment down to 7.9 percent as of June 1999 (from 12.3 percent in 1979) but blacks also were more likely than whites just a decade ago to hold professional and managerial jobs.

Blacks remain the most chronically unemployed and underemployed segment of the American labor market. The disparity in employment opportunity between whites and Blacks has become a recurring statistic in the U.S. economy. The average "white" family today owns nearly ten times the property and other assets the average black family owns.

For all the frenzy surrounding affirmative action, and the portrayal of corrective measures as preferential to Blacks and Hispanics, Blacks continue to face unemployment twice that of whites.

Despite decades of rhetoric from Republican and Democratic presidential administrations regarding expanding economic opportunity in the United States, people of color, mainly Blacks, remain locked out of the labor market.

The Bureau of Labor Statistics of the U.S. Department of Labor reported the nation's unemployment rate at 5.6 percent. Black unemployment stood at 9.8 percent compared to 4.9 percent for whites. It was a slight improvement over figures for January when Black joblessness was 10.5 percent.

Black male unemployment for February was 9.4 percent compared to 8.8 percent for females. Younger Blacks fared no better; unemployment for Black teenagers between ages 16 and 19 years old was 25.1 percent and the labor force participation rate among Black teens was just 28.3 percent.

The numbers only tell part of the story. The U.S. economy has been in a such a slouch that many Americans simply ceased trying to find work. Last month there were 484,000 Americans who fell into that category. Another 1.7 million Americans were not counted as unemployed because they had stopped actively searching for employment in the four weeks prior to the Bureau of Labor Statistics survey.

This news comes against the backdrop of the U.S. presidential election and the increased attention to the issue of "outsourcing" or the movement of American jobs offshore. As many Americans cope with the prospect of long-term unemployment, and white-collar professionals experience their first taste of being excluded from opportunity, the loss of jobs to foreigners is becoming an explosive issue.

Therefore, it is even more important that those Blacks who have the capital hire other qualified Blacks. It is also important that their "black dollars" penetrate Black businesses and invest in new start up Black businesses. The more economic growth power we invest in ourselves including Black candidate campaigns the more economic power we will have as a group. Once we identify qualified Black American candidates for president we have to be ready to back them economically.

To look at black American leadership past and present it is important to give you an idea the types of Blacks that I feel could actually win and most definitely be taken as a serious candidate for the presidency. The following Black Americans (and the list is not inclusive) are examples of individuals in my opinion that have the character, education and experience that a black candidate could use as role models in order to be taken seriously as a candidate for president. My example sections were based on their demeanor, national exposure, education and experience and their respect across all cultures. Remember; as you view these examples reflect on the past United States Presidents their experience and education levels. The last thing any of us want to read or hear in the media is that the Black choice is not qualified regarding experience and education. This has been stated in the past when former Blacks ran for the presidency.

Let's now review some examples of past and present Black Americans who have **earned** the respect to be examples of what qualifications the first Black President of the United States must obtain to become a serious candidate.

Dr. Condoleezza Rice

Dr. Condoleezza Rice became the Assistant to the President for National Security Affairs, commonly referred to as the National Security Advisor, on January 22, 2001.

In June 1999, she completed six-year tenure as Stanford University's Provost, during which she was the institution's chief budget and academic officer. As Provost she was responsible for a $1.5 billion annual budget and the academic program involving 1,400 faculty members and 14,000 students.

As professor of political science, Dr. Rice has been on the Stanford faculty since 1981 and has won two of the highest teaching honors — the 1984 Walter J. Gores Award for Excellence in Teaching and the 1993 School of Humanities and Sciences Dean's Award for Distinguished Teaching.

At Stanford, she has been a member of the Center for International Security and Arms Control, a Senior Fellow of the Institute for International Studies, and a Fellow (by courtesy) of the Hoover Institution. Her books include <u>Germany Unified and Europe Transformed</u> (1995) with Philip Zelikow, <u>The Gorbachev Era</u> (1986) with Alexander Dallin, and <u>Uncertain Allegiance: The Soviet Union and the Czechoslovak Army</u> (1984). She also has written numerous articles on Soviet and East European foreign and defense policy, and has addressed audiences in settings ranging from the U.S. Ambassador's Residence in Moscow to the Commonwealth Club to the 1992 and 2000 Republican National Conventions.

From 1989 through March 1991, the period of German reunification and the final days of the Soviet Union, she served in the Bush Administration as Director, and then Senior Director, of Soviet and East European Affairs in the National Security Council, and a Special Assistant to the President for National Security Affairs. In 1986, while an international affairs fellow of the Council on Foreign Relations, she served as Special Assistant to the Director of the Joint Chiefs of Staff. In 1997, she served on the Federal Advisory Committee on Gender — Integrated Training in the Military.

She was a member of the boards of directors for the Chevron Corporation, the Charles Schwab Corporation, the William and Flora Hewlett Foundation, the University Of Notre Dame, the International Advisory Council of J.P. Morgan and the San Francisco Symphony Board of Governors. She was a Founding Board member of the Center for a New Generation, an educational support fund for schools in East Palo Alto and East Menlo Park, California and was Vice President of the Boys and Girls Club of the Peninsula. In addition, her past board service has encompassed organizations as Transamerica Corporation, Hewlett Packard, the Carnegie Corporation, Carnegie Endowment for International Peace, The Rand Corporation, the National Council for Soviet and East European Studies, the Mid-Peninsula Urban Coalition and KQED, public broadcasting for San Francisco.

Born November 14, 1954 in Birmingham, Alabama, she earned her bachelor's degree in political science, cum laude and Phi Beta Kappa, from the University of Denver in 1974; her master's from the University of Notre Dame in 1975; and her Ph.D. from the Graduate School of International Studies at the University of Denver in 1981. She is a Fellow of the American Academy of Arts and Sciences and has been awarded honorary doctorates from Morehouse College in 1991, the University of Alabama in 1994, the University of Notre Dame in 1995, the Mississippi

College School of Law in 2003, and the University of Louisville in 2004. She resides in Washington; D.C. Dr. Rice credentials alone exclude her from being a token in the Bush administration. She is qualified and based on her education and experience the opportunity inbeing the first African American appointed as National Security Advisor deserved. No democrat president in history has ever appointed an African American in a powerful position as National Security Advisor until President George W. Bush. Actions speak louder than words.

General Colin Powell

President Bush nominated Colin L. Powell on December 16, 2000 as Secretary of State. After being unanimously confirmed by the U.S. Senate, he was sworn in as the 65th Secretary of State on January 20, 2001.

Prior to his appointment, Secretary Powell was the chairman of America's Promise - The Alliance for Youth, a national nonprofit organization dedicated to mobilizing people from every sector of American life to build the character and competence of young people.

Secretary Powell was a professional soldier for 35 years, during which time he held myriad command and staff positions and rose to the rank of 4-star General. His last assignment, from October 1, 1989 to September 30, 1993, was as the 12th Chairman of the Joint Chiefs of Staff, the highest military position in the Department of Defense. During this time, he oversaw 28 crises, including Operation Desert Storm in the victorious 1991 Persian Gulf War.

Following his retirement, Secretary Powell wrote his best-selling autobiography, *My American Journey*, which was published in 1995. Additionally, he pursued a career as a public speaker, addressing audiences across the country and abroad.

Secretary Powell was born in New York City on April 5, 1937 and was raised in the South Bronx. His parents, Luther and Maud Powell, immigrated to the United States from Jamaica. Secretary Powell was educated in the New York City public schools, graduating from the City College of New York (CCNY), where he earned a bachelor's degree in geology. He also participated in ROTC at CCNY and received a commission as an Army second lieutenant upon graduation in June 1958. His further academic achievements include a Master of Business Administration degree from George Washington University.

Secretary Powell is the recipient of numerous U.S. and foreign military awards and decorations.

Secretary Powell's civilian awards include two Presidential Medals of Freedom, the President's Citizens Medal, the Congressional Gold Medal, the Secretary of State Distinguished Service Medal, and the Secretary of Energy Distinguished Service Medal. Several schools and other institutions have been named in his honor and he holds honorary degrees from universities and colleges across the country.

Secretary Powell's distinguished credentials make him qualified to lead our country. As an African American he worked hard to achieve these credentials they alone exclude him from being a token as some African Americans state. If he were a white man no one would say he was a token but because he is a black man doesn't he deserve the same respect from his people as African Americans around this country give Clinton? No democrat president in history has appointed an African American as Secretary of State except for George W. Bush. Actions speak louder than words!

Late Dr Martin Luther King Jr. January 15, 1929-April 4, 1968

Born Michael Luther King, Jr., but later had his name changed to Martin, Martin Luther attended segregated public schools in Georgia, graduating from high school at the age of fifteen; he received the B. A. degree in 1948 from Morehouse College, a distinguished Negro institution of Atlanta. After three years of theological study at Crozer Theological Seminary in Pennsylvania where he was elected president of a predominantly white senior class, he was awarded the B.D. in 1951. With a fellowship won at Crozer, he enrolled in graduate studies at Boston University, completing his residence for the doctorate in 1953 and receiving the degree in 1955 In Boston.

In 1954, Martin Luther King accepted the pastor position of the Dexter Avenue Baptist Church in Montgomery, Alabama. Always a strong worker for civil rights for members of his race, King was, by this time, a member of the executive committee of the National Association for the Advancement of Colored People. Early in December 1955, he accepted the leadership of the first great Negro nonviolent demonstration of contemporary times

in the United States, the bus boycott described by Gunnar Jahn in his
presentation speech in honor of the laureate. On December 21, 1956, after
the Supreme Court of the United States had declared unconstitutional the
laws requiring segregation on buses, Negroes and whites rode the buses
as equals. During these days of boycott, King was arrested, his home was
bombed, he was subjected to personal abuse, but at the same time he
emerged as a Negro leader of the first rank.

In 1957 he was elected president of the Southern Christian Leadership
Conference, an organization formed to provide new leadership for the now
burgeoning civil rights movement. The ideals for this organization he took
from Christianity; its operational techniques from Gandhi. In the eleven-
year period between 1957 and 1968, King traveled over six million miles
and spoke over twenty-five hundred times, appearing wherever there was
injustice, protest, and action; and meanwhile he wrote five books as well as
numerous articles. In these years, he led a massive protest in Birmingham,
Alabama, that caught the attention of the entire world, providing what
he called a coalition of conscience. And inspiring his "Letter from a
Birmingham Jail", a manifesto of the Negro revolution; he planned the
drives in Alabama for the registration of Negroes as voters; he directed
the peaceful march on Washington, D.C., of 250,000 people to whom he
delivered his address, "1 Have a Dream", he conferred with President John F.
Kennedy and campaigned for President Lyndon B. Johnson; he was arrested
upwards of twenty times and assaulted at least four times; he was awarded
five honorary degrees; was named Man of the Year by *Time* magazine in
1963; and became not only the symbolic leader of American blacks but also
a world figure.

At the age of thirty-five, Martin Luther King, Jr., was the youngest man to have received the Nobel Peace Prize. When notified of his selection, he announced that he would turn over the prize money of $54,123 to the furtherance of the civil rights movement.

On the evening of April 4, 1968, while standing on the balcony of his motel room in Memphis, Tennessee, where he was to lead a protest march in sympathy with striking garbage workers of that city, he was assassinated.

Though Dr. King unfortunately is no longer with us, he was the type of Black American that would be taken seriously as a candidate for the presidency. No matter the heat in fighting a social war he never flip-flopped in his beliefs, he wouldn't sacrifice his non-violence techniques nor would he be silenced. Dr. Martin Luther King Jr. demonstrated for Black Americans a powerful leadership that has never been replaced in American history.

Former Ambassador Andrew Young

Ambassador Andrew Young is an ordained minister in the United Church of Christ. He has published two books, <u>A Way Out of No Way,</u> Thomas Nelson, and <u>An Easy Burden</u>, Harper Collins. His awards include the Presidential Medal of Freedom and many honorary degrees. He served three terms in the US Congress from the 5th district of Georgia. In 1977, President Jimmy Carter named him Ambassador to the United Nations. He served two terms as Mayor of Atlanta and was Co-Chairman of the Centennial Olympic Games in 1996.

Ambassador Young was a top aide to Dr. Martin Luther King, Jr. during the civil rights movement, was involved in its inception, and served as Vice-President of the Southern Christian Leadership Conference. He presently serves on the Board of the Dr. Martin Luther King, Jr. Center for Non-Violent Social Change.

Ambassador Andrew Young is chairman of Goodworks International, a specialty-consulting group based in Atlanta, Georgia, that provides strategic services to corporations and governments operating in the global economy. He serves as a member of the boards of directors of numerous organizations and businesses including Delta Airlines, Argus, Host Marriott Corporation, Archer Daniels Midland, Cox Communications, and Thomas Nelson Publishers.

Now the National Council of Churches' Immediate Past President, Ambassador Young served as NCC President — a part-time, non-salaried leadership post — in 2000-2001. His NCC presidency brought him full circle, as he had served as associate director of the Department of Youth Work of the NCC's Division of Christian Education from 1957-61.

Congressman Harold Ford Jr.

In time, as he develops and becomes more seasoned Congressman Harold Ford Jr. (Son of Harold Eugene Ford), a Representative from Tennessee will be considered as a serious candidate. Prior to the presidency he would be smart to consider running for the senate or even governor to place himself as a serious contender to be a vice president consideration or a major cabinet appointment. Born in Memphis, Shelby County, Tenn., May 11, 1970; graduated from St. Albans School for Boys, Washington, D.C.; B.A., University of Pennsylvania, Philadelphia, Pa., 1992; J.D., University of Michigan Law School, 1996; staff aide, United States Senate Committee on the Budget, 1992; special assistant, United States Department of Commerce, 1993; elected as a Democrat to the One Hundred Fifth and to the three succeeding Congresses (January 3, 1997-present).

Congressman Harold Ford Jr. has the ability as a Democrat to cross American cultures. Along with his education and experience he presents himself well. His demeanor commands respect and he represents extremely well. Congressman Harold E. Ford, Jr., (TN-09) was sworn in to represent the Ninth District of Tennessee in 1996 at age 26. Ford represents a new generation of political leaders who seek to replace the partisan politics of the past with fresh ideas and a pragmatic approach to the challenges of the twenty-first century."

He is not trying to live in the shadows of his father but is his own man with his own ideas and stands on his beliefs allowing his own "new" ideas to represent America.

Late Congresswoman Barbara Jordan[2]- 1936-1996

Barbara Charline Jordan was my personal role model, a great lady, born in Houston, Texas. Barbara was the first to serve in the United States Congress because she was the first African American woman from a southern state. Barbara was traveling in segregated buses sitting on the seats labeled colored to attend college at Texas Southern University. Barbara graduated from Texas Southern University and received a law degree from Boston University. Barbara was earnest in her belief that she could make her mark.

Her accomplishments as a lawmaker are outstanding. Barbara began practicing law in her hometown of Houston and became a country judge assistant.

In the Democratic Party in the 1976 Barbara Charline Jordan became the first black keynote speaker at a National Convention of the party. Barbara was a Texas Democrat, was a member of the House of Representatives from 1973-1979. Barbara listened in awe as Edith Sampson a black woman lawyer from Chicago spoke.

She was the first black to hold a seat there since 1883. In 1979 Barbara became a professor at the Lyndon B. Johnson School of Public Affairs at the University of Texas. Later she was elected to the Texas state senate committees. Barbara ran for congress and became the first black to be elected from the deep south since the turn of the century. She served three successful terms of office. Of her accomplishments, many civil rights leaders wanted Barbara to join them in their organizations to fight for justice for African Americans. But seeing herself as a lawmaker first and foremost, Barbara preferred to make changes within the legal and governmental system. Barbara has been a professor at the University of Texas since 1979. She is currently the special advisor on ethics to the governor of Texas.

Her approach was to respect the humanity of everybody. A prime example of what a serious candidate for the presidency would be as an African American.

There are many more African Americans that would be taken seriously as a candidate for the presidency of the United States. These that I have mentioned are favorites of mine who I feel would be taken seriously. Not because they are Black Americans but because of their level of education, experience, demeanor, respect and the ability to cross cultures in America. These examples of men and women; who through their examples promotes hope proving the unthinkable that the American dream can be achieved through hard work, sacrifice, educational achievement and life experiences even through the obstacles of racism.

Education/Career Choices as we race to the White House

Though many past presidents had law degrees, today a person has more education options if not interested in law. Some of the educational options would be obtaining a minimum of a master degree in public policy or public administration with an undergraduate degree in political science. Our current president George W. Bush has a Masters in Business Administration (MBA). If you are not interested or do not have a law degree consider either a PHD in Political Science, Public Administration or Public Policy as an alternative. Either would be a plus along with political experience.

Political experience also does not mean you have to become a political official. Remember to run the country you need business experience. Believe it or not Chief Executive Officers of top corporations really run the country not the president, Congress or Senate Representatives, these are simply "figure heads". Most political officials are already bought out by the special interests (Corporations) that finance the politician's campaigns. Below is a list of some of the careers that would help give you the experience to run for the presidency:

- Presidential Cabinet Appointment
- Military Officer Careers
- Political Campaign Opportunities
- Foreign Affair Careers-Executive Level
- University Professor
- CEO of a Corporation proving leadership skills
- Successful Business Owner
- National Elected Congress or Senate Office
- Law
- National Security Career-Executive Level
- FBI Careers-Executive Level
- Lobbyist and Interests Group Careers
- International Relation Careers-Executive Level
- Journalism Careers

In order for a black to be taken seriously as a presidential candidate the obstacle in not being qualified must be removed. If not, the press will either eat you alive exposing your ill qualifications if you don't have the necessary education and experience or they will completely ignore you as a serious candidate. If you possess the education and competent experience they will have to at lease respect you as a serious candidate.

Obtaining the Nomination- How Delegates Choose Candidates in Presidential Elections

Would a Black American Have a serious chance? As the race continues to the white house it is important that the proper steps are taken. Unfortunately, the way the political system is in this country even though qualified, capturing a major parties nomination for an African American will not be easy. The politics are thick and people interested in a political career will learn fast that in politics you have no friends or enemies. It all depends on the issue at hand and the daily personal agendas you have to deal with. Friends become enemies and enemies become friends overnight depending how your agenda will help their cause. I remember when I was elected for a position in civil rights; a lawyer friend at the time said "make your friends before you need them."

Before a candidate is able to take part in a presidential election, the candidate must acquire the support of enough delegates during the presidential primary season. This has only ever been accomplished by a "white", male. To have a serious African American candidate for president they **MUST** be able to win the privilege to represent their Party in the general presidential election. In order to win the presidency the candidate must become either the Democrat or Republican Parties nominee to really be taken seriously in the race.

It is important to understand what delegates are to the political process. You would think that during the primaries which are held in each state, that the voters choose the parties nominee but they do not. Delegates are equivalent to Electors in the Electoral College. When you vote in a presidential primary or caucus, you are really voting for a person who pledges to vote for your candidate at the national convention where the nominee is chosen officially. How those delegates are selected varies, to some extent, from state to state and Party to Party.

The ways in which we vote in primaries need to change. First of all there needs to be open primaries in every state. What this means is that even if you are registered as an independent you would be able to vote in a primary election. Some states have open primaries but we need to accomplish this in every state giving every voter the freedom of choice to cast their vote for the candidate they support not based on the political party. It should be unconstitutional to prevent any citizen of the United States from exercising their right to vote. The way the system is today an African American would have to be selected over "white" rich males in both the Democrat and Republican primaries by the voters and then by the delegates. This is almost impossible to do since the delegates and the voters mostly white are the majority. The other obstacle is African Americans usually back white candidates. I am a firm believer that just because you are a black candidate doesn't mean that blacks should always vote for black candidates especially if they are not qualified. I also do not believe that only one black should run for a position. If you are qualified let the best person win. There are always the pros and cons on splitting the "black vote" for more then one candidate and the white candidate slips in. It can happen in some situations but let's face it for the presidency an African American candidate needs more then the African American vote to win. The below article clearly discusses the issues surrounding African Americans obtaining the support of other African American politicians. Most Black American Politicians who have won political races primarily run and win in a large percent of African American populated communities. In order to be a serious contender for the presidency you must have a multicultural appeal to voters.

The Black Caucus

Many black politicians back white Democrats. In the first presidential contest in more than a decade in which Black Americans were running, Rep. Eddie Bernice Johnson, D-Texas, offered no apology for endorsing Sen. John Edwards, white, as the Vice President choice of Senator John Kerry of the Democrat Party.

Black Caucus members primarily Democrats focus on their party winning therefore, continually reward white Democrat politicians with their support. Many of the Black Caucus members probably felt that the two Blacks who ran in the in the 2004 presidential election primaries had a lot of baggage and realistically could not win

A former chairwoman of the Congressional Black Caucus, wasn't the only prominent black Democrat lining up early behind white candidates and not in support of the Rev. Al Sharpton or Carol Moseley Braun, the only black woman ever elected to the U.S. Senate.

A Detroit News survey of the 39-member caucus — the Democratic political muscle of the black community that consists of the black members of the U.S. House — found two members supporting Braun and one "leaning" toward Sharpton.

That's a dramatic contrast to 1988, when Black Caucus members solidly lined up behind the Rev. Jesse Jackson, who won a number of key states — including Michigan. Jackson leveraged his power to advance issues of concern to African-Americans at the convention. The key word here is issues of concern. Your message must be about the issues that each American faces in order to be considered a serious candidate. Jackson focused on issues of concern primarily for Blacks today, a Black candidate must be able to launch a message that represents issues of all cultures and being able to articulate clearly those issues, with solutions, will be the key.

Understand that when Jackson ran the Black Caucus unity only came after Jackson's strong showing in the 1984 presidential contest, when Black Caucus members scattered their support among many Democratic candidates.

Sharpton I am sure was upset and probably blasted the promising pattern of Black Caucus endorsements; identified them as a "losing approach" in gambling on what might win that has never paid off for black America. Many Black Caucus members didn't think the black candidates were taken seriously therefore they had no faith in either of them winning.

20 years later, what can those caucus members who went with John Glenn, Gary Hart or Alan Cranston say they got for their endorsement? Blacks had political election breakthroughs as Doug Wilder being elected governor in Virginia, David Dinkins being picked New York's mayor, and Ron Brown being named chairman of the Democratic National Committee, all of them are Black Americans.

As I was growing up I used to hear people say they think we all look alike. That statement has been proven wrong, not only don't Black Americans look alike we are not alike. Trust me in saying it is going to take a certain style and grace along with the education and experience, a communicator that can appeal to all Americans as the commander in chief as we race to the White House with a black candidate who will be taken serious. .

Of the 15 Black Caucus members who made endorsements, four favored Edwards of North Carolina, three backed Sen. Bob Graham of Florida, three supported Sen. John Kerry of Massachusetts, one wants former House Democratic leader Dick Gephardt of Missouri, and one was for Gen. Wesley Clark. All of those candidates are white.

Michigan's two Black American members of Congress, John Conyers and Carolyn Kilpatrick, both of Detroit, didn't endorse quickly as the others though it was reported that Kilpatrick's office said she likely will after the Detroit debate on Oct. 26. They were smart not to follow the crowd.

Paula Diane Harris

They underline game plan was for Black Americans to gamble speaking primarily about the Congressional Black Caucus endorsements. At the annual caucus conference in Washington, D.C., black members of Congress and other attendees pointed to a number of reasons they thought Sharpton and Braun drew few endorsements.

These range from Jackson's already proven record — he had received 3 million votes in the 1984 campaign, which prompted Congressional Black Caucus members to get behind him in 1988 — to a single-minded practicality to pick the perceived strongest candidate to go up against President Bush.

Realism, for example, was why powerful Charles Rangel of New York, the ranking Democrat on the tax-writing Ways and Means Committee, stated he came out for Clark.

In news interviews, Rangel has said Clark's military background is Teflon to the question of being a patriot— a key asset, Rangel argued, in blunting any advantage Bush may have on military issues.

Others at the conference pointed to the tradition of supporting presidential candidates from one's own state. Rep. Frank Ballance, D-N.C., for example, had stated that he thought "highly" of Braun and Sharpton but decided to join the rest of the North Carolina delegation in backing Edwards of their home state. Still others said race wasn't the determining factor driving their candidate preference.

One caucus member had stated, "Martin Luther King Jr. wasn't telling white people not to stand beside him." Millender-McDonald of California stated to a news media that she endorsed Sen. John Kerry of Massachusetts because of their work over the years on children's issues.

The Black American community needs a leadership to be sensitive to their needs. Millender-McDonald, the chairwoman of this year's caucus conference felt a white person could do that as well as a black candidate.

I feel the early endorsements of many candidates diluted the influence of Black Caucus members in this presidential election. They acted too fast with endorsements.

The caucus members instead should have withheld their endorsements until a nominee was picked. This strategy would have had more clout to get promises on key Black American concerns, which should have been their focus since they were not going to back either black candidate. It is important to note that because you are black doesn't mean all black people have to vote for you. As a black candidate you too should earn the black vote. Members of the Black Caucus should have held out to ensure the issues affecting black America got on the platform of whomever the nominee would be which in this case is John Kerry. Again, because they jumped too quickly black issues have become lost in this presidential election.

Some have argued that if the caucus came out and said they were backing the black candidates it would be a different ballgame. The other candidates would know they have to go to that particular black candidate. The question is can we get a lot more bang for the buck if everyone endorses one person? In this presidential election I would have to say no because of the qualifications and baggage of the black candidates. They didn't have a chance. The Black Caucus should have used the strategy to not endorse until after the nominee was clear and focused on the issues that affect black Americans in this country.

By the caucus spreading endorsements over many candidates, candidates didn't feel in my opinion the need to focus on key issues like racial disparities in prison sentencing, educational opportunities, health and wages. This was a big mistake.

It was also assumed that there was a sense that even some caucus members assumed the black candidates couldn't win because America isn't ready to elect a black president. I disagree. I think there are black Americans as we discussed previously that have the demeanor, education and experience that would be elect able and or at least would be a serious candidate. But it takes the right candidate with the appeal to be able to cross cultures with the right amount of experience and education.

Braun felt according to her comments to the media that she wasn't given the benefit of the doubt that she could have won an election having been elected to the U.S. Senate. There is still a sense that as a black American, there is a climbing battle to be taken serious.

Black Americans need to begin running in white communities and not only in primarily black communities. Blacks elect whites and whites can elect blacks to represent them. Blacks don't all live and work in black communities therefore they don't always have to run in black communities. There are other avenues a person interested in politics can gain experience in public service. Ron Brown, former Chair of the Democrat Committee is a great example of another road to take. If you decide not to run for an elected office an appointment by a president to a major cabinet position is another option. There are different opportunities but you need to prove longevity in the political field in some capacity. Keep in mind that you need to work your way up which will not only develop you personally but will prove your qualifications and experience. It takes hard work, sacrifice and patience with strategic planning. Don't expect to become another Senator John Edwards only being elected one term in the Senate and now the Vice President choice of the Democrat Party. It doesn't usually happen that easy even for white man. Be prepared as a black candidate for president to pay your dues in public service.

What in my opinion held back Braun and Sharpton was more the sense that they didn't have the formidable political and or education credentials of their opponents than that they couldn't win because they are black. I predict the first Black American president will have credentials similar to either Colin Powell, Secretary of State and a former general, or Dr. Condolezza Rice, National Security Advisor. Other options could be serving as governor, vice president, national senator, or appointment to a major cabinet position.

To black American college students, internships equate to experience. Begin to build your experience as you are completing your education. Internships working on presidential campaigns, employment in major political party offices like the Democratic and Republican Committees in Washington DC, and positions in a congress or senate office are invaluable experiences. Don't be afraid to grow slowly, only be afraid of standing still. Keep in mind no one owes you anything because you were born a Black American and that includes their vote. Earn your way, which is the best way taking nothing for granted. Making the right choices in your life together with hard work and sacrifice, taking education seriously and believing in yourself; these are the qualities that will allow you to earn your seat at America's table of decisions. Never use poverty or your race as an excuse for poor character. Remember it is the lessons learned from each and every mistake you will make along the way that will ultimately lead you to your successes in life.

Another change that needs to be made in order to have more of a serious chance in the primary to obtain the title of a major party nominee is that all states should have the same primary election day like the general election. This would prevent the first state to vote, which is Iowa, to determine who wins the election. As we saw in the 2004 democrat primaries every other state followed the lead of the first two states Iowa and New Hampshire. By the time the primary gets to the last state in the primary as in the case of the 2004 Democrat primaries, the primary for the presidency was over. A good example is Pennsylvania. Their primary is April 27th but the democrat primary had been over with months prior to their primary election leaving one candidate, which was John Kerry. There were no choices because the other candidates had dropped out due to not coming in first with the previous state primaries.

For illustrative purposes regarding how states choose their delegates, let's focus on the Democrats since they had more than one candidate running in the primaries for president in the 2004 election.

All of the fifty state Democratic Parties and those representing the District of Columbia, Puerto Rico, American Samoa, Guam, the Virgin Islands, and Democrats overseas have the flexibility to determine how their delegates are determined as long as their process falls within the guidelines of the Democratic National Committee.

Regardless of how states choose delegates, the Democratic National Committee uses a standard formula to determine how many delegate votes each state will get at the presidential nominating convention.

In addition to the base delegate votes, each state (and D.C.) is awarded a number of pledged "Party Leaders and Elected Officials" delegate votes equal to 15% of the number of Base delegate votes as determined by the "Allocation Factor" x 3000 formula described above.

All base delegate votes are pledged to a particular candidate. Prior to the first meeting of the National convention states (and jurisdictions) conduct primary elections, caucuses, or conventions to give Democrats a chance to vote for their preferred nominee.

Democrats use a proportional method as opposed to the winner-take-all system used for the Electoral College. Each candidate is awarded a number of delegates in proportion to their support in the state caucuses or the number of primary votes they won.

Going into national conventions, an overwhelming percentage of the delegate votes are known. How non-pledged or super delegates will vote is more of a mystery. Each state is assigned a certain number of this kind of delegate votes for Senators, Members of Congress, Democratic Governors, current and former Democratic Presidents and Vice-Presidents, past Democratic congressional leaders, and retired Party chairpersons. This group of people can endorse a candidate at any time but unlike pledged delegates they can change their vote as often as they choose to before they vote at the nominating convention.

This year there are 4,317 delegate votes to the Democratic National Convention. To win the party's presidential nomination, a candidate needs at total 2,159 delegate votes or two-thirds of the total number when the final votes are tallied. Sometimes this system does not work perfectly. When that has happened in the past Party leaders made deals and compromises to select a nominee.

Can a candidate win the nomination without winning the majority of the primary votes in each state? Yes, but not likely. That is why a serious black American candidate in order to be taken seriously MUST appeal to a multi-cultural base of voters and be able to cross the color line.

As identified in previous chapters in order to be a serious black candidate it will take more then standing up at a podium announcing your candidacy. You now have an idea how the political system works to capture the crown in becoming a major party nominee. Sound impossible, it's not. You just need the right stuff!

Public Speaking- The Black American Candidate

There is a difference between public speaking in a presidential race and preaching from a pulpit. Mastering communications verbally is essential. Bill Clinton and Ronald Reagan are two examples of political figures that mastered communications. My favorite was Barbara Jordan. When Congresswoman Jordan spoke not only could you understand every word she said, but she made you feel as though there was a rainbow of hope, that she was speaking right to you personally, a brilliant speaker. Public speaking is a gift and many politicians do not have this strength.

Your goals are to master public speaking to the point that your speech is clear and that you can articulate the issues. I have nothing against a good sermon, however, regarding politics and issues people face everyday, they don't want to be preached at they want you to be able to communicate on their level of understanding.

Remember, even though you are a black you are not running to be the Black president of the United States but rather to become a president for all citizens in fulfilling your promises in the "peoples" House" of America. Communication is the key!

There are theories that challenges black speech that a half century of social-linguistics theories took a new look at the history of the controversial and highly visible ethnic English dialect Ebonics, also known as African American Vernacular English (AAVE). The book, titled "The Development of African American English," was written by Dr. Walt Wolfram, William C. Friday Distinguished Professor of English, and Dr. Erik Thomas, associate professor of English. The book concludes that earlier African-American speech was much more regional, but that it coexisted with language roots from its African heritage.

If older black Americans and older whites in Perry County sound similar, the speech of younger Perry County Black Americans couldn't be more different. This is because black speech became strongly identified with a sense of black identity in the 20th century. Simpler put, younger blacks don't necessarily want to sound like whites. Good English (and not that all whites speak it because they do not) has no race or color. Black students must learn the American language and speak and write it with pride.

I don't know about you but I was born in America. I went to American public schools along with whites. Besides a southern style speech opposed to a northern style dialect how different should a white person speak opposed to an African American?

Make no mistake that in order to become a serious contender for the presidency your speech must cross American cultures and be clearly understandable. If they are going to find a joke about you on the Dave Letterman show do not let it be your speech, dress style, body language, education or experience.

Between the B-bop music, and rap, the music industry would never win awards for articulation. Have you ever listened to a song but couldn't understand a word the singer sang? Sometimes you can pick out a word here or there that is understandable but for the most part it is difficult. This not the kind of example of articulation you want to master. Don't worry either that because you are educated and speak good English that your Black American sisters and brothers make comments similar to "you talk like a white person". Tell them from me "I don't know what a white person talks like, but I am proud to speak with distinction my American language. I'm proud to be an American".

We have done our children harm with some approving Ebonics which is a slang. The only part of the white house you will get in speaking Ebonics is either in the kitchen, maid service or the gardens if you are lucky. You must to be able to speak the English language and write it. I know it sounds cool and chillin. It's so chillin that it will freeze your Black American buttocks right out of "white collar" opportunities and most definitely the presidency. Slang examples to avoid are:

EBONICS

A slang dialect used by certain groups of the black American community.

Yo, Big Daddy upstairs,

You be chillin

So be yo hood

You be sayin' it, I be doin' it

In this here hood and yo's

Gimme some eats

And cut me some slack, Blood

Sos I be doin' it to dem dat diss me

Don't be pushing me into no jive

Ang keep dem crips away

Cause you always be da man, G

Straight up.

Aa-men.

Get the point!

Let's face it there are perceptions out there that Black Americans can't speak clearly and unfortunately in many instances (especially our young people) it is true. We are also known to be Baptist preachers raising the roof with bible versus, stumping up and down on the alter, raising our voices that would shake the first five rows in attendance. Hands waving, wiping the forehead, eyes wide - you know what I mean. No one likes a good sermon more than I, but in the political field that's not the image you want to project.

As stated earlier not many politicians of all races can speak but an African American running for president, people will pay attention to your every word that is a guarantee. You have to master the art of public speaking, because in any leadership position, especially the presidency, you must be able to communicate effectively. Not only will the American people need excellent communications from you but your staff will as well. If you are able to master the skill of communication it will set you apart from the rest of the pack and people will not focus on your color but on your speech technique. Remember an old expression; it's not what you say but how you say it.

After you master the English language and public speaking it is equally important that you are able to fluently articulate legislative and foreign affair issues to people who are voters that have different levels of education. To be able to master the English language being able to clearly articulate your messages will be in your favor.

Many politicians are labeled with "they do not answer questions." Instead they talk around the question. To get a voters attention you need to master how to respond to open and closed ended questions. Let me explain the difference:

Open Ended Questions versus Closed Ended Questions

Open Ended Questions allows for a spontaneous response. The response can be contrasted to a multiple choice. An example would be **ended** - having come or been brought to a conclusion; "the harvesting was complete"; "the affair is over, **ended,** finished"; "the abruptly terminated interview"

Closed Ended Questions are those questions, which are answered finitely by either "yes" or "no." Also known as dichotomous or saturated type of questions. Closed-ended questions include presuming, probing, or leading questions. By definition, these questions are restrictive and are answered in a **few** words.

As you are speaking, remember your body language. You don't want your mouth to give one message and your body language another. Practice looking in the mirror, videotape yourself, playing it back to pick up on where you need to improve. Become your best and hardest critic. It is important to be able to speak on your feet answering questions without loosing your composure no matter the subject matter. Public speaking is an art and most politicians are terrible at it. The competition is not that keen to beat. The Black American candidate that masters it will be the dazzle of every voter.

Shows like the David Letterman show use situations showing politicians in embarrassing situations their body language versus their verbal communications actually make comic acts out of these situations. I've seen it done with former President Bill Clinton when he addressed the nation regarding his affair with Monica Lewinsky. I've also seen it done to George W. Bush when he had his televised press conference in April 2004 with the national media who asked if he made any mistakes on the war on Iraq. I've seen it with John Kerry when he was reminded that he voted for the war on terror and now he has flip flopped his position. Losing complete control of body language and voice control was more interesting then what they had to say. Remember eye contact - don't avoid the inquirer with your eyes, when responding look them straight in the eye.

A good introduction for a politician you don't want to earn is:

I'll begin by telling you what a remarkable person our candidate is. Now I'll describe all the wonderful things they've done for the community. And I'll conclude by saying some things that are true.

Chapter II

Taken for Granted?

Prior to the Iowa Caucus on John Kerry's web site for president was a category of "Activist Communities"

Black Americans for Kerry

Prior to the Iowa Caucus Senator John Kerry's campaign web site included an area of support for communities. Under that link the web sites included the NAACP, National Urban League and Rainbow Coalition all of them 501(c)(3) tax-exempt organizations. Having these organizations on the democrat senator's campaign web site gave the impression that black Americans were endorsing John Kerry for President.

The key concern is that even though we say that the Democrat Party take blacks for granted, they couldn't do it without the help of black organizations as the NAACP, Urban League and the Rainbow Coalition promoting white democrat candidates by placing their organization web site links on a democrat candidates campaign web sites.

According to the Internal Revenue Service (IRS) there are exemption requirements. To be tax-exempt as an organization described in IRC Section 501(c)(3) of the Code, an organization must be organized and operated exclusively for one or more of the purposes set forth in IRC

Section 501(c)(3) and none of the earnings of the organization may inure to any private shareholder or individual. In addition, it may **not attempt to influence legislation as a substantial part of its activities and it may not participate at all in campaign activity for or against political candidates**.

Julian Bond, Chairman of the NAACP made recent statements regarding the Republicans. The NAACP being a 501(c)(3) organization placed their web site link on John Kerry's campaign web site prior to the Iowa Caucus. This action did in fact attempt to influence black Americans to vote for Senator John Kerry opposed to President Bush. The IRS needs to do a better job in making sure that tax-exempt organizations stay within the regulations. If not, then they should loose their 501(c)(3) status.

Bond, who has been chairman of the NAACP since 1998, accused Bush of trying to starve the government of money through tax cuts. He said social programs aimed at minorities have suffered as a result.

Perhaps the NAACP needs to consider becoming a for-profit business opposed to non-profit. This would enable them to not have to follow 501 (c) (3) regulations and allow them to contribute as a business paying taxes. Their taxes would then help the federal budget regarding social programs they feel are necessary for minorities.

John Kerry received a 100 percent rating from the National Association of the Advancement of Colored People (NAACP) and the Human Rights Campaign for his work in support of civil rights during the 107th Congress. This is the same man who doesn't take black American candidacy for president seriously. This is the same man who the NAACP clearly supports along with the Urban League and the Rainbow Coalition having had their web addresses on his campaign web site even before the Iowa Caucus.

Yet not one of these organizational leaders came out and protected black American dreams that our young people and young professionals can aspire and one day become the first black American President of the United States. To me their silence indicates clear evidence that we need new leadership in these organizations that supposedly are suppose to be representing black Americans in this country.

Where was the leadership of the NAACP and the Urban League? Rev. Jesse Jackson ran for the presidency himself in 1988, he alone should have publicly denounced Senator Kerry's remarks but instead they chose to ignore it. Why because Kerry is a democrat?

How will a black American become a serious contender for the highest office in the United States?

Senator John Kerry who may become our next president proved he has no respect for Black American leadership but he continues along with the Democrat Party to court the black vote, taking it for granted with the help of civil rights organizations. Kerry says he wants to change America, he's been a career politician for many years, what has he been doing all of this time? Why doesn't he stand on his voting record in this election on issues like the Iraq war? For Kerry's statement he made to the Urban Radio, I give the national civil rights organizations NAACP, Urban League and Rainbow Coalition an "F" for failing to stand up against his statement protecting black Americans right to equal opportunities.

July 2004 was the NAACP's National Convention. John Kerry was there waving his arms high telling the black Americans in attendance he won't forget them at the white house as their president. His grin was wide as he shook hands with Mfume as hundreds of black Americans in Philadelphia were led by the NAACP to spend millions of black dollars in white hotels making them richer and backs poorer. Black dollars were also spent in mostly white businesses and restaurants making them richer and blacks poorer sending black delegate's home with the same problems they came with. The speeches were grand but civil rights leaders continue to wear suits of "sold out" for the black American communities.

The NAACP especially has become too political as a 501c3 non-profit organization with many 501(C)(4) local branches across the nation.

Julian Bond, NAACP Chairman grouped all Republicans calling them names making statements as," Republicans appeal to the dark underside of American culture'. This was wrong and unacceptable. The NAACP preaches racial neutrality and practices racial division. Since this is the way the leadership of the NAACP feels about all Republicans then every single Republican should request their membership fees back and cease to be members of the organization. If Republican's are not good enough then neither should be their money.

The NAACP continues to prove how irrelevant they are to the needs of black Americans. In 2002, Republicans for the first time outspent

Democrats in campaign dollars on black-owned radio. With Generation X and younger, black voters are three times more likely to be conservative than their parents. More and more black Americans are realizing they do not need the guidance of the NAACP leadership or other non-profit civil rights organizations to move forward. Blacks are becoming more conservative.

It is definitely time for Black Americans to wake up and smell the coffee with civil rights organizations that have become extensions of the Democrat Party and fight for open primaries in every state. Every Black American needs to change their voter registrations to independent making political parties **EARN** their vote especially the Democrat Party who takes Black American votes for granted! If any party should have a Black American nominee you would think it would be the Democrat Party because of black Americans voter loyalty to the party. Black Americans at least deserve the party's respect. There is no doubt that the black American vote is crucial to the 2004 presidential election for the democrats to obtain victory.

Congressman Jesse L. Jackson, Jr. (D-IL-2) congressional office in Washington DC communications director sent a press release to the Andrew Young Center National Center for Social Change Inc. for us to post on our web site. The press release was in regards to Senator John Kerry selecting a black American running mate. Congressman Jesse L. Jackson's press release that went out national stated the following:

"Sen. John Kerry must now select a running mate. Conventional wisdom suggests it will either be a moderate-to-conservative white male southerner or a moderate white male mid-westerner. Granted, conventional wisdom is sometimes wrong.

There is also the view that "Democrats take the black vote for granted and Republicans write it off."

If the media ask Sen. Kerry, "Will you put a progressive African American on your ticket?" It would be appropriate from him not to answer. If ask, "Would you consider the same?" He would easily say, "Of course."

Instead of those questions the media should ask him to analyze this:

There approximately are 37 million blacks in the U.S. Approximately 25 million are eligible to register and vote by age and citizenship. Between 14-15 million are registered, but only 11-12 million actually voted in the 2000 presidential campaign. The most room for growth in voter registration and assured Democratic voter turnout is in the African American community!

While, by definition, all presidential campaigns are "decided in the middle," the ticket helps to determine where that middle is. There is one "middle" for a conventional wisdom ticket, another for a Kerry-McCain ticket (as some have suggested), and yet another for a Kerry-"credible progressive African American" ticket. The center for the first and second would be to the right of the third because the latter would send many more Democratic voters to the polls.

Most pundits are suggesting, because the electorate is so polarized, this year's presidential election, more than most, will be a "base vote" election - that is, the party with the best turn out of its hardcore supporters will win. Again, I'm suggesting that the largest and most loyal - but most underutilized - voting base in the Democratic Party is African Americans.

In 2000, Gore won 20 states and the District of Columbia for a total of 267 electoral votes. Bush won 30 states and 271 electoral votes. Because of redistricting - which shifted seven electoral votes into Bush's red states - winning the same states in 2004 would total 278 electoral votes for Bush and 260 for Kerry.

A progressive African American should be on Kerry's ticket for hard, cold, politically calculated reasons - not out of any benevolence, paternalism or doing African Americans a favor. It would give Kerry the best chance at an Electoral College victory, and be in the Democratic Party's best interests.

In terms of electoral votes, it would help Kerry in all 20 states (and DC) Gore won in 2000. Of the 16 toss-up states, it would help in half: Arkansas, Florida, Michigan, Missouri, Nevada, Ohio, Pennsylvania and Wisconsin - a total of 117 Electoral College votes. Why? Because those states have significant black populations - ranging from 15.7 percent in Arkansas to 5.7 percent in Wisconsin who would be motivated to register and vote for such a ticket. Who else could Kerry run with that would put more states in play?

In addition, an African American on Kerry's ticket would also give Democrats their best opportunity to win back control of the House. Of the 36 House seats in play, 29 have significant numbers of black and/or Hispanic voters.

A progressive African American on the ticket would also give Democrats their best chance of maintaining seats, winning Republican seats, and taking back control of the Senate. Democratic Senate seats most vulnerable in 2004 are in Florida, Georgia, Louisiana, North Carolina, South Carolina and South Dakota. Fifty-three percent of all African Americans live in the South, but are massively unregistered - seven million. Among the most vulnerable Republican Senate seats are Illinois (where Kerry will be riding an African American's coattails, Barack Obama), Kentucky, Missouri and Pennsylvania.

It would also do the most to complicate the Republicans' most anticipated strategy - that Kerry will select a conservative-to-moderate white male for his ticket. With an African American on the ticket, Republicans could no longer take the South for granted. While Democrats may not win everywhere, Republicans would have to compete by putting money, time and effort in over a dozen southern states from Texas around to Virginia.

If the Republican Party played the race card, and they certainly would try - using coded language as welfare, law and order, affirmative action, crime, the death penalty or something entirely new - as they have always done since the 1964 "states' rights" campaign of Goldwater and Nixon's "southern strategy" in 1968, a progressive African American candidate would easily recognize it, be able to appropriately interpret it to a broader American public, and a significant number of more tolerant white socially moderate swing voters would resent it and not be as inclined to vote for them. Finding the balance that appeals to their conservative race conscious base while appealing to their more moderate race tolerant voters would be made more difficult for Bush and the Republicans with a credible African American on the ticket

Some will argue, "Now is not the time to engage in a risky strategy!" Actually, now is the time because Democrats are highly motivated to un-elect Bush with whatever vehicle is necessary. It's also the least risky strategy because we are guaranteed it would maximize the Democratic vote, benefiting the Democratic presidential, House and Senate candidates.

Others may fear a potential racial backlash. In 2004, fears are overrated, with the most recent example being the Illinois campaign of Democratic Senate nominee Barack Obama, a progressive African American and Harvard Law graduate. The frontlash - that is, a massive increase in Democratic voters going to the polls - would outdistance any backlash.

And if it did not end Nader's campaign, it would largely negate it, as many progressives inclined to support him would abandon a hopeless third party effort if there were a progressive African American on Kerry's ticket.

The word "progressive" is deliberately inserted to indicate that any African American VP candidate would have to have a progressive economic record and not be limited in appeal by being (overly) identified with issues that are perceived (rightly or wrongly) as "for blacks only." The campaign's focus must be on economic common ground issues, not on divisive racial ones.

In 1988, after George H.W. Bush selected Dan Quayle as his running mate - a person many saw as unqualified - there were several studies that concluded the American people vote for President, not for Vice President. That is true for the vast majority of Americans, and it is true for black Americans unless one was on the ticket. In that case, while many Americans would be concentrated on the top of the ticket, Black Americans would be focused on both. Democratic voter registration money would be more effectively spent as African Americans and other progressives would register and vote in massive and unprecedented numbers.

Finally, who? I suggest Bobby Scott (VA) or Mel Watt (NC) would be excellent candidates. Both have law degrees - Bobby Scott from Boston College and Mel Watt from Yale University - and both are constitutional experts. Both are from the South and from districts with large white populations - Rep. Scott's is 40 percent white and Rep. Watt's is 45 percent white - so they know how to appeal to white southern voters.

The analysis speaks for itself. Kerry would win the election with a progressive black running mate. And, with a bold political strategy, he would win a place in history for himself, the Democratic Party and democracy itself".

A great thought from Congressman Jackson but of course as loyal as black America is to the Democrat Party including Congressman Jackson (D), John Kerry chose Senator John Edwards from North Carolina as his

Vice President choice. Al Sharpton received the consolation prize that was a few minutes to speak in prime time at the Democrat National Convention. How we sell out so cheaply!

There are no questions that the Democratic Party cannot win without the support of black voters in 2004. Black Americans through voting must begin to send a message at the polls to the Democrat Party that no longer will they accept their votes taken for granted. Their first step is to change their voter registrations to either an independent status or another party's choice. Black Americans are the most loyal block of voters the Democrat Party has, supporting it in numbers that far exceed their percentage of the U.S. electorate. . In 1996, Bill Clinton trailed Bob Dole among whites 46 to 43 percent, but got 84 percent of the black vote and won the election. In 2000, Al Gore won an historic 90 percent of the Black vote, which was critical to his success in the popular vote. Given the increased polarization of the electorate and the disappearing "swing voter" in 2004, Black voters are more important than ever and Kerry knows it!

The Democratic Party rewards black voters with backing dependent federal and state programs that in my opinion help keep them dependent on the system. We need to become independent of these government programs succeeding more in education so we can obtain the higher paid jobs with health insurance benefits. Black Americans themselves can turn it around by having more graduates from high school and college to being more qualified to compete for the higher paid jobs. This achievement will decrease sentencing to prison terms due to inappropriate choices. Due to lack of education allowing drugs to life decisions. Blacks must begin to take responsibility for their choices and for the choices of their children when they are dependent on their parents. Family involvement is the key in decreasing juvenile delinquency and academic failures in school. No president can correct all of these issues but if we accept our responsibilities individually, making better choices, our quality of life will improve.

As a society we can fight discrimination when you are qualified and you were kept from the opportunity because of race, we can fight racial profiling, we can fight employment discrimination, we can fight housing and credit discrimination and other racial issues. But to improve our quality of lives we have a responsibility as well to ourselves. We can't win the battles when you are not qualified due to not performing in school, we can't win the battles when you chose drugs over work, we can't win the battles when unprotected sex was a choice and now we are faced with aids, we can't win the battles when we condone teenage pregnancies as parents, we can't win the battles when we choose to buy our children high priced sneakers and cloths instead of a computer, we can't win if we continue black on black crime and violence in black communities . We can't blame the government for our own personal choices. Poverty is not an excuse for poor character and not all of us are poor. Many blacks doing very well economically as well as having done and are doing the right things giving our children the tools they need to succeed in America. But too many black Americans are not doing what they need to do as parents.

There are many whites as well that are not the best parents but our children have it hard enough just being black, they can't carry our mistakes and ill choices as well. A mind is a terrible thing to waste and out there somewhere is the first black president of the United States of America. We have a responsibility as a people to recognize that one child left behind is one too many. No politician will tell you what I just said, no civil rights organization will tell you either, but it is time we faced some things together as a people in order for us to continue to grow becoming even greater protecting our strong legacy that helped build and shape America.

A Democrat, the late John F. Kennedy once said, "Ask not what your country can do for you but rather what you can do for your country". He sounded like a Republican but he was a Democrat. As a Black American as you begin to prepare to cast your vote for the president of the United States in November you will ask yourselves what has the Republicans done for me? Also ask yourselves what has the Democrat Party done for you? The answers may be the same but the main question you should be asking is what have I done for myself, my family and for my community?

How did we get to where we are? Why are Black Americans loyal to the 'white Democrats who won't support any black Americans for President to become their party's nominee? The party itself has few if any visible black Americans in paid leadership positions that the average person would know their name at their headquarters in Washington. Even though for the most part black Americans have been programmed to hate the Republican Party, can they make the argument of what the Democrat Party is doing for them today? Do many black Americans know the history as to why so many have register democrat? Let's take a trip down memory lane.

President Franklin Delano Roosevelt, in his first term, had an official group of African American advisors. This circle of mid-level officials in positions throughout the government in Washington came to be known as the "Black Cabinet".

Harold Ickes, the head of Roosevelt's Public Works Administration, had been chairman of the Chicago NAACP before he joined the administration. Eleanor Roosevelt, the president's wife, served on the national NAACP Board. Between 1933 and 1935 Ickes and Mrs. Roosevelt brought to Roosevelt's attention prominent African Americans they thought worthy of appointment to federal positions.

1935, Dr. Mary McLeod Bethune, head of the National Youth Administration and president of Bethune Cookman College, convened the first meeting of the African American Roosevelt appointees.

The 'Black Cabinet" primary concern was that African Americans would not be denied the benefits of "New Deal" programs set up to help people through the Great Depression. Unfortunately, the 1930's were a time in history of survival not a celebration of diversity and contribution. The history books have not been kind in letting people know about the "Black Cabinet".

For decades, African Americans have been involved in politics in both major parties and selected in appointments therefore, we have earned our right to be taken seriously even as a presidential candidate.

President George W Bush in appointing Condoleeza Rice, Alberto Gonzales, Mel Martinez, Colin Powell and Rod Paige to his cabinet President-elect Bush took steps towards "Acknowledging the support of all of my black and Latino voters." In a press conference he explained that every single one of his Black and Latino voters would be rewarded with a seat in his cabinet. President Bush kept his promise.

Why is President Clinton popular among black Americans?

For one thing, blacks have concluded that his empathy is not just rhetoric. In his two administrations, he has appointed more African Americans to cabinet posts than all of the previous U.S. Presidents combined. Among them: Agriculture Secretary Mike Espy, Commerce Secretary Ron Brown, Labor Secretary Alexis M. Herman, Energy Secretary Hazel O'Leary, Transportation Secretary Rodney Slater, Veterans Affairs Secretary Jesse Brown and Assistant Secretary of State for African Affairs Susan E. Rice. His only appointments for the position of Surgeon General have been African Americans (Jocelyn Elders and the current surgeon general, David Satcher). No president before Lyndon Johnson appointed any black to the Cabinet. Only four Black Americans have served on Cabinets since Johnson and prior to Clinton's first election. Indeed, Clinton has surrounded himself with African Americans. His policy initiatives have been sensitive to this community. He still supports some form of affirmative action. Although he ultimately supported the 1996 Welfare Reform Bill, he resisted dynamic changes in welfare policies and was uneasy about the passage of this bill. He was the first American president to initiate a national dialogue on race relations in America. He was also the first American president to tour Africa.

On an episode of Bill Maher's "Politically Incorrect," the legendary music producer, Quincy Jones, stated that no other president in his lifetime has been able to connect and relate to the African American experience like Clinton. Perhaps this connection is best captured in the movie, "Primary Colors," starring John Travolta as a president clearly intended to parody Clinton. In this movie, the president is depicted as a person who grows up with African Americans in a small Southern town and becomes intimately connected to the black experience.

Senator John Kerry if he becomes the United States President in 2004, in his Senate office there are no African Americans hired. He has no idea what it is like to be a poor "white" citizen in this country let alone an African American. African Americans must not let anyone capture our votes. We must begin to be more selective in who we choose to give our vote regardless of their political party affiliation. Not every Democrat is a friend to Black America and not every Republican is an enemy. Black Americans must vote accordingly on who the candidate is and what they stand for NOT continue to be loyal to a specific party anymore. Make candidates EARN your vote by making them stand on their records and the issues you face everyday.

If there were a time that Black Americans should re-examine their value to the democrats, it is now. Blacks gave Al Gore 90 percent of their votes. Contrary to some black loyalty to the party, it was understandable as a rational decision once Bush campaigned at a racist college, refused to criticize the Confederate flag, and chose in Dick Cheney a running mate who once voted in the House against a resolution to call for the release of Nelson Mandela from jail in apartheid South Africa. No one saw Bush as clearly as the blacks when he used to govern in Texas. Black Americans there gave Bush only 5 percent of their votes. Let's face it the choices now in 2004 aren't good either way you go.

But Bush has done something that no other president in history has and that is he named Black Americans Colin Powell as Secretary of State, Condoleezza Rice as National Security Adviser and Rod Paige as Secretary of Education. These people are not tokens they are qualified Black Americans who took a seat at the democracy table of decisions. President Clinton didn't do that and Kerry won't!

Whether people think these black people pursue policies more friendly to the Confederate wing of the Republican Party or to Black Americans in general, they are qualified for the job and were given the opportunity to lead in this country. We already know that Powell supports affirmative action and a woman's right to choose and it has absolutely no impact on Republican policy. But even with that fact he hasn't changed his position on these issues.

That said, the Republicans have still one-upped the Democrats, who probably have never given a thought to a black person running foreign affairs. The irony is that it is has been easier for Bush to promote his choice of Black Americans, with no fear of offending white voters, than it has been for the Democrats, who spend as much time weeding out Black Americans they fear would offend conservative white suburbanites.

President Clinton had black American secretaries of commerce, labor, agriculture, transportation, and energy, but he also spent considerable time dumping Lani Guinier, Joycelyn Elders, and Henry Foster. Clinton appointed more Blacks to mid-level posts opposed to Bush appointed more Blacks to cabinet major posts. Clinton also punished the Black poor with punitive welfare reform and by maintaining racist drug laws that continue to disproportionately throw Blacks into jail.

It cannot be forgotten that Clinton, while playing Black American ministers like a saxophone, originally elevated himself in the minds of white suburbanites in the 1992 race by humiliating Jesse Jackson and going home to Arkansas for the execution of a brain-damaged Black man. You really have to research the facts.

After nearly seven decades of overwhelming support for Democratic presidential candidates, no Black candidate for even vice president is in remote sight. The party, in its own paternalism, has groomed no Powell or Rice. One of the most absurd examples of how black American support was so taken for granted was when Al Gore picked Joseph Lieberman as his running mate. Lieberman, head of the Democratic Leadership Council, known as the Republicrats, had to spend relentless time at the Democratic convention convincing Black Democrats that he really did not mean it a few years ago when he said it was time to rethink affirmative action. As in the case of Senator Kerry's remarks it seems as though for some reason blacks forgive the white democrats for their comments but see the Republicans as bigots when many of the Democrats feel the same way as the Republicans.

By now, the conservative Democrats have felt that Gore lost the election because he was too much of a supporter of rights. That is odd since Gore, who won the popular vote, might have won Florida if he would have demanded to count all the questionable votes in predominantly black districts.

If conservative Democrats tried to bring the party even more to the right, it is time for black voters to abandon the Democrat Party ensuring their votes will be earned in the future. Change is always difficult and takes time to be accepted by people. Blacks have been programmed to think the Democrat Party is in their corner when in reality if they could pull more votes from the southern states they would dump blacks and not care if they voted or not. My preference is for Blacks to begin to take their voting registrations out of the Democrat Party and evenly place them in the other political parties. Eventually, blacks should register independent and we need to lobby to have open primaries in every state. This way all politicians would have to earn the vote!

What is plain is that no group in American politics has gotten so little in return for their support than blacks. It has gotten to the point where, we can rightfully be accused of a slavish, even stupid, loyalty to the Democrats.

Thanks to civil right leaders today they have helped make blacks believe that there is no place for them in the Republican Party. Blacks have been programmed in believing that the Republican Party is a bunch of bigots and do not care about black issues. This is not true. Yes we disagree on issues with the Republicans but I don't agree on all of the positions in the Democrat Party. More troubling is many voters have no idea due to not being educated what the positions are for either party. When you go to the polls you shouldn't be voting for a party or who looks like a president or the media's choice and or who the civil rights leaders are telling you to vote for. You need to know the issues, research the candidates. Did you ever hear the saying 'God bless the child that has his own"? I'm now talking about common sense. My mother used to say "God told the people he was giving out brains and some thought he said trains and many got on board without their brains"! People were given the a mind to make choices, think for yourself don't allow others to make choices for you.

Blacks no longer can afford to be confused and must begin to vote for the candidate regardless of their party's affiliation, the candidate that best represents our issues not the candidate that uses our issues to get elected. There is a difference! We also must face a painful fact and that the leadership of the past civil rights movement under Dr. Martin Luther King Jr. is gone and it was a leadership that has not been replaced. The civil rights leaders today have prostituted civil rights for their own personal gains. Yes, I do mean the NAACP, Rainbow Coalition and several more. It's sad and painful to accept but it is a reality and the white people already know it; it is time we accepted it. Perhaps at one time leaders such as Julian Bond, Rev. Jesse Jackson and Kweisi Mfume actually did fight for civil rights but along the way their price was found and they sold the black voice for personal gain and power. The leadership in the White House is very important regarding the issues like the next Supreme Court appointments, but in this election blacks will loose either way. Blacks must become more concerned about the leadership in the black house and it needs to be replaced. Even though Al Sharpton would like to become the 2nd Rev. Jesse Jackson Sr. he is not the answer for black leadership. Sharpton is too eager to be seen and is very easily distracted and bought like a used car. He would just be another Rev. Jackson, Bond and Mfume, all in bondage by choice.

America Speaks

After my response to Senator John Kerry's remark regarding earning the right to become the 2nd Black President I received hundreds of emails and letters. I think it is important for people across our nation to read the responses from everyday citizens white, black, Indians Asian, a melting pot of different diverse cultures male and female. I have included those of support as well as non-support.

Ms. Harris,

I am proud to be your fellow citizen. I was appalled that some referred to President Clinton as the first black president for exactly the reasons you so eloquently express. When those who are consistently treated condescendingly and taken for granted rise up with you and demand that candidates earn their individual votes, we will see major changes immediately implemented by candidates in both major parties.

I did not grow up even close to economically privileged, but I know, that as a Caucasian child, I grew up privileged by comparison. Your call for an apology from Senator Kerry for his remarks, to every black child, many of whom have the abilities to be an effective U.S. President as an adult, but will lack the opportunity to be the candidate of either major party, is inspiring and patriotic.

-Len

Ms. Harris,

I am sure there are many things you and I would disagree about. I am a conservative Republican from Tennessee. I am also a white man. However, I can only say that to add context to my remarks.

Let me say that I was pleasantly surprised to see your response to Senator Kerry's pandering remark about wanting to become the "next black president".

As you so clearly pointed out, he is a rich white man who is almost as clueless about my life experiences as he is about yours. I believe that as a white man, I can never really know what most black people have, do now, or will face in their lives. But at least I'll readily admit that!

In my opinion, it is unfortunate that so many black people ignore this gross display of arrogance from Senator Kerry and former President Clinton. I believe their arrogance extends to their policies. They push government dependence and operate with an air of "I know what's good for you" that is repugnant to me. I just wish we Republicans were given half a chance to prove that limited government, lower taxes, more personal and family responsibility coupled with vigorous enforcement of existing equal rights laws, could yield better outcomes for ALL of us, including black Americans.

I believe all Americans would do well to read and actually study what Dr.

King spoke and preached about: Equality, Opportunity, and Fairness. I can be for all these things alongside you, without pandering and saying I could ever truly understand what it is like to live your life.

Respectfully,

Bryan

The Democrat Party is the modern plantation owner. I am a Native American that has learned that democrats are only interested in our vote. They have been promising the same things for 40 years. It is time for all minorities to wake up and see what the democrat party is really like. They want to own us. In 1964 Lyndon Johnson said speaking to democrat supporters "we can buy and sell the Negros and they will never know it". I for one am tired of being bought and sold. How about you? Had enough of the democrat's lies???????

Fred

Ms. Harris, thank you for asking for an apology from John Kerry regarding his "second black president" remarks. It seems that many black people don't understand that he's attempting to emotionally manipulate them by making a statement, which implies similarity. As you pointed out, his life's experience is anything but commonplace (to a poor white person, let alone a poor black one).

I'm sure that he has concluded that most blacks will never be any the wiser about his privileged background until after they help him get in the White House.

Too few "black leaders" speak out about this, but then again many don't want to cut their purse strings.

Thanks for your courage!

Patricia

Sometime we have to know when to pick our battle. Would you preferred to have "Bush" 4 more years for President. Give "Kerry" a break!!!!!! Yes, we are would love to see a black President but at this point… we have to look at reality…I feel that "Kerry" is the only one that could beat Bush at this point. The country is in such a bad state right now and we need to focus on issues that are important and not something as small as a comment. I respect your views as well but we have to focus on what is good for us. I feel you need to start with the comedians on "BET" which made the comment that President Clinton was the first Black President. Thanks, for writing…regardless…I think your organization is doing wonderful work. God Bless.

-Penelope

I just wanted to say how disappointed I was to see Diane Harris's campaign about John Kerry's remarks about wanting to be "the second black president". Obviously, I would love to see a real black president in office —

and some day we will — but it was so sad to hear your remarks. It DOES NOT help us.

Dear Paula Diane,

I appreciate your comments, too. I think there is so much at stake this year — the Supreme Court for example — that we all need to work hard and be strategic.

Thank you for writing back. I wish you and Andy well with your work.

Kevin

Hello Ms. Harris:

It was a rather intellectual commentary wasn't it? I respect your not being familiar with my writing style. The simple truth is that any black person, who believes that a white man who is worth hundreds of millions of dollars is a man who wants to be known as a black president, is either quite blind with stupidity or is the most gullible person on the face of the earth.

Allow me to establish one credential. I wrote the book that formed the foundation of the plan put forth by President Clinton. It was not his wife's plan. I care about the future of America and that ALL Americans be treated equally. The Democrats have proven over and over again that they do not. Enough said. Best wishes.

Dennis

Amen, you are one of my new heroes.

I have a theory that when God divided human language at the Tower of Babel, one of the lesser-known languages that keep people apart is the language that politicians speak. I have been embarrassed by some of the Democratic politicians, not just republicans, when they claim to speak for those who are struggling and need a helping hand. Notice I said helping hand, not slap in the face. You have my prayers. I pray three times a day for my own soul, and the souls God has given into my keeping, love, and friendship. I will be happy to include your fight for justice as well.

The Lord is with you.

Bill

Ms. Harris,

I find it very unfortunate that you would use your strong voice to bring attention to the statement made by Senator Kerry in regards to his "earning the right to be the second black President". He was obviously speaking lightly - in an obviously non-racial manner - about the Black Community; its relationship with Bill Clinton and how he would like to follow in those footsteps in actions. This was completely blown out of proportion. I'm a professional Black male in the Semiconductor Industry. I'm also born and raised in West Philly. Personally, I took no offense to what Mr. Kerry said. Obviously a person can't please all of the people all of the time so that's why you wrote your letter. I also completely understand and respect your point. However, I also think being that Mr. Kerry is obviously not a racist there is no need to react in an over sensitized manner. Is that statement going to make you reconsider whom you vote for? Are you going to vote for George W Bush? Do you think he will miss during a 2nd pass at Affirmative Action?

My point is this. The World Economy has been here officially for about a decade. As long as we are the World Superpower the decisions we make will affect every life on Earth - not just yours and mine. That said - We couldn't trust the power of this Country to the current Administration any longer. So therefore we all need to work united behind and supportive of Senator Kerry in his bid for the White House. You could have made your point known privately through direct communications and helped to effect change within their Campaign without giving Republicans a laughing point or swing voters any reason to change their mind. You may not want to buy this point but I assure you one thing. Senator Kerry saying a stupid remark meant to help his Blue Blood background mentality to identify and/or connect with our Community is much more acceptable than 2 more Wars, soaring gas prices, horrible economy, high unemployment, possible cancellation of Affirmative Action, overturning of Roe v Wade, destruction of our Environment - and the list can go on. Your Organization has enough respect to be able to get a meeting with their Campaign. You probably would've brought more opportunity and business to AYNCSC that way as well. When you are working with friends, family, community, businesses etc it is always to use honey before vinegar. I was told once to be firm on your values but supportive in actions. Well that applies now more than ever.

It's time to unite and work together in getting this sitting President out of office. I assure you I'm no political activist or some Kerry Groupie - but I am a very concerned African American with what I see happening in OUR World today. I also completely disagreed with you statement and felt you would appreciate seeing a different point of view. Besides that I would also like to Thank you for what you and your Organization does. I wish you all of the best in everything you do and hope that we all can realize a color blind but culture rich society in our life times.

Best regards,

Ron

Los Angeles, CA

I wanted to say that as an American Indian/ half white, I know discrimination as much or more than anyone. I completely agree with you on Kerry's' arrogant manner a condescending attitude.

It is true, as you stated. "There is only one race. The human race." and furthermore, we are all Americans. I don't like the term "African American" because if you were born here you are an AMERICAN period. White African nationals who moved here have tested the term. So let's forget the presumption of racial profiling. It exists and the black population too and, in that sense, encourages it.

Why is it that if I get a summer tan I'm an Indian and in the winter, when I lose the tan, I'm more acceptable? I don't care....

136

I am an AMERICAN and that's the colors I see when I look in the mirror.

Sincerely, James

Dear Ms. Harris:

I don't know who you are but whoever you are, your statements lambasting John Kerry is providing support for the Right-wing Republicans and hurting your effort to raise money from Blacks and progressive Whites who is probably your base of support. Your statement(s) about John Kerry was unnecessary, ineffective, and clearly demonstrated that you are very lacking in political savvy; unless, of course, you were paid by the Republican Party. Since most African Americans/Blacks knew what Mr. Kerry meant by patterning himself after Bill Clinton, Ms Harris's ignorant statement(s) was repeated all day long on the right-wing radio and television programs. She also probably was able to convince some Blacks and Independents who are apolitical or uneducated to vote for George W. Bush in a Presidential election that is expected to be closer than the last. Until I hear a public retraction of her statement(s), I will never support the Andrew Young Center for Social Change, nor will anyone whom I can contact over the next year or two.

Zack

Montgomery, AL

Your request of an apology from John Kerry is a cheap way to reap publicity. I can only assume after your stunt that you must support Bush's re-election. I read your biography (autobiography?) and could not find any time of your life when you were not at the public trough.

Shame on you!

Dick

If this is the best thing you can do to get media attention, it's real sad. Find something of more substance to comment on or be quiet.

Clinton

Politicians from both parties, Rep and Dem, are from wealthy, privileged families. On any issues, was Clinton really any different then Bush? No. We have to go back 100 years to see any real differences in the parties. Both only care about two things, themselves, and being elected. Both equate to power and ego. They will do anything necessary to get them. If they cared about "blacks" or "whites" or "the people", they wouldn't be taking billions of dollars from special interest groups. Our country would not be held hostage by corporations. I have lost faith in both parties. I probably won't even vote this time, and if I do, it will be for Nader. I don't care if I am throwing away a vote; at least I will feel better about it.

Bill

With all due respect, I think your wasting your time as well as the money that supports your causes when you bring those such as John Kerry to the table on racial issues. As a gay man I know all about oppression as my people to get treated as nothing less then second class. I would encourage you to generate some of that energy towards getting Bush out of office and generating a voter drive instead of bringing to light issues that aren't there. I don't understand why you would even consider adding fuel to Bush's fire unless of course you decide to back Nader.

Good Luck in your endeavors peace

Madison

You are correct in that I missed your point from the perspective as you explained it. I do know that racism and / or the daily black experience is not understood or apparent to whites. In fact, there is a subtle superiority bias built into TV, advertising, etc. everyday everywhere. To actually counteract, or neutralize, the racism toward black people practiced up to this point would include massive, generous reparations as well as complete apologies and acknowledgments. To me, black militancy as per the Panther party was natural progression, easily understood. And I still cannot know of living with the indignities and disrespect that is part of black life in America.

However, as exclusive/unenlightened as the comment from Kerry could be interpreted, I believe his heart is in a much better place as compared to the alternative. From a white who is adept at sassing out true attitudes in other whites.

Dear Paula Diane,

I appreciate your comments, too. I think there is so much at stake this year — the Supreme Court for example — that we all need to work hard and be strategic.

Kevin

Until you are born black in America and have walked in our shoes you will never earn the right as a white man to be called a black president. GoooooooooooooooooPaula!

James

Well said. Best of luck to you.

Bill

I disagree with Ms. Harris' reaction to the statements made by John Kerry. Ms. Harris' statement that because Kerry is a "privileged white man" he has no idea what its like to be a black man in America does worse than miss the point — it is a divisive statement at best, at worst it is racist.

The point is that even privileged white men CAN understand what its like to be a poor black man in America. Privileged white men, and everyone, even privileged black men, can learn to appreciate what it is like from meeting and talking with poor black men, from reading what is written about the subject (the subject is well covered, from stoic academia to the first person), from being a part of public service work, etc. If Ms. Harris truly believes privileged white men are inherently incapable of such understanding, her world view is (a) rather dim, and (b) must also accept the natural correlatives — whites can never learn to understand the lives of blacks, nor can browns understand the lives of reds, nor reds of yellows, and so on.

Ms. Harris might also note that John Kerry has a 100% rating from the NAACP on civil rights legislation. -Ronald

---

Dear Ms. Harris,

You are absolutely correct. Mr. Kerry is a man of privilege. For Mr. Kerry to capitalize on the history of social injustice to blacks by pretending to care for blacks is shameful. Furthermore, you are asking the right questions, "Where are the leaders of the black community denouncing his comments?" He wouldn't know the life of a middle class American, much less a poor American.

I wish you and your organization a great deal of success. Your approach to social injustice is a novel idea, I wish you well.

John

Long Beach, CA

Please pass this on to Diane Harris:

I worked for then Congressman Andy Young's office in the spring of 1973 as his first intern.

I just wanted to say how disappointed I was to see Diane Harris's campaign about Joh Kerry's remarks about wanting to be "the second black president". Obviously, I would love to see a real black president in office — and some day we will — but it was so sad to hear your remarks. It DOES NOT help us.

Kevin

Thank you for keeping our candidates accountable.

Peace,

Chip

Dear Ms. Harris,

I applaud your voice in speaking out against John Kerry's "2nd black President Statement". I was shocked when I first heard of his comments. I remember thinking…when was the first? Your editorial was thoughtful and inclusive of ALL races, and further illuminates the racial divide the Democratic Party has been trying to manipulate. He should concentrate on earning votes rather than taking an ethic group's vote for granted.

Thank you for speaking out when an outrageous political comment like that is made.

Sincerely,

Debra

This is a blatant grab for concessions. Have you no shame?

Ron

Hello,

My name is Dennis and I am a conservative Republican. The best man at my wedding is of African heritage He has been a dear friend for over 20 years. His name is Fred and I tell him that the only time I know he is black is when he tells me. He sadly buys the empty promises of the liberal lies. My tax advisor is not only of African heritage but wears dred locks (sp). We laugh at how I am a big fat middle-aged white guy and he looks like Ziggy Marley.

It is truly sad to see how so many in the black community continue to support Democrats when they continue to abuse the trust of so many in the black community with false promises. What have they ever delivered? Never mind, they just make promises that sound good and apparently that is good enough for organizations like yours.

The difference between leftist organizations like yours and swarmy deviate conservative white Republicans like me is simple enough to explain. I actually took the words of Martin Luther King to heart and you do not. Let me remind you with what Reverend King said (paraphrased)

"Don't judge a man by the color of his skin. Judge him by the content of his character."

I do and you don't. That is why you will never see any change. All you can do to stay alive is spew more hatred against people like me. For that I am sad.

I close by challenging you to really promote change.

God Bless.

Dennis

Paula

Thank you for the quick response. Personally, I'm not in favor of Kerry, or any candidate that tries to be something they are not, and in my opinion, I feel Kerry was doing just that. He could have said the first Chinese President; it would have been the same to me. It's politics as usual, regardless of race.

As far as BET, I'm just saying that the double standard exists, and although it's not right, it's there. How does a nation move forward if the different races continue to preach unity, but create their own groups?

Eric

Hello, I would like to post this message in response to your organization's response to John Kerry's statement that he would like to be the next "Black President." As an African-American woman, and law student, I think it is cool that he wants to build upon the legacy of Bill Clinton and the affinity that the black community has for Clinton by becoming the next "Black" President. Black people love Mr. Clinton, at least most of the ones in may family and the friends that I know and so it seems like a good thing to me that Kerry would like to make that inroads into building coalitions and community in the way that Clinton was able to. Sure Mr. Clinton was a cheating bastard, but he is human, and in the end all his craziness was just plain funny because it was so patently ridiculous, unless you are Hillary, of course.

It seems as if you are picking a battle that makes your organization seem stuffy, uptight, and focused on the wrong agenda. Why is it that you are so quick to cry racism when in fact Kerry's comment was made publicly and was intended to be lighthearted?

Please do not dilute the legacy of Andrew Young by picking silly battles. It does no good to anyone. Sure John Kerry is rich and knows nothing about being black - everyone knows that, but that is not the point. The point is that he was making the connection to being like Bill Clinton in the eyes of the African-American public. In fact, it makes me like him even more.

Choose your battles wisely, it just makes your organization seem out of touch to take something funny and turn it into a racial issue. Just some thoughts from a black person who was not offended at all by Kerry's statements.

Sincerely,

Cerita

I believe one of the problems with most organizations is they; they are selfishly motivated for power, money and ego boost. It looks like the days of selfless leadership like Dr. Kings are gone.

All of you seem to concentrate on simple remarks without knowing the intent for publicity, while larger issues. Obviously your stand is one of those against John Kerry's simple remark.

I am appalled that Andrew Young is tolerating this nonsense. Since I live in Atlanta, I know of his work. Do you really think, your remark addresses any real issue such as education, caring for the elderly, making youngsters responsible, respected productive citizens of the society? These are what I call social change and making progress.

Everything else is utter nonsense and tells the world how silly and myopic one is.

It appears African Americans are the ones bringing up color of the skin more and more.

What did Dr. King say in his "I Have Dream Speech", maybe it is time for every one to go back and read it again. Every time I read it, I get chills. Now that is vision, selfless leadership for change.

Let us not loose site of the bigger picture here folks.

Paul

Atlanta, GA

Good for you Ms. Harris.

It's about time that someone spoke up concerning Kerry's remarks.

Rusty

If you think that was offensive towards us then you are speaking as a solo isolated uneducated voice. While President Bush has the military (over represented by African Americans) killing men of color in a war that is at its very least illegal and while Bush befriends the Trent Lott's of the world who would love to bring back Jim Crow you choose to zero in on this. Your memory is somehow short circuited if you think the comment Kerry made (indecently to champion the cause of civil liberty) was offensive. Please read your history books and your newspaper to see how this President is making us suffer economically and making us suffer from lack of civil rights more than ANY other President. Martin Luther King would be shipped off to Guantanimo Bay as a terrorist if he dared march today. You should be ashamed of yourself for letting the ENEMY use your child like rantings for their own ends. Resign your post or just zip it if you can't think before you blabber.

Grubaker

You know in these times of unnecessary bickering and looking at issues that really mean something, your ordinance regarding Kerry's remarks repulses me. All Americans can find someone or something said that offends them. It is time everyone toughens up, understands words for their deeper meaning and not their surface interpretation.

Do you actually believe that any man black or white in today's society would make a remark that would insult a potential vote if they are running for president.

Ted

Why make an issue out of this Kerry thing… Chill out, I'm sure you have more important issues on the table…

M. N.E.

Dear Paula,

Do you really think that John Kerry's "black president" remark was worthy of such a strong reaction from you? In my opinion, his words were not only harmless, but intended to reach toward the black community. It seems to me that this constant taking of offense serves no one.

Best Regards,

Scott

Ms. Harris, I read your criticisms of John Kerry and I have to shake my head. There are many issues to address in the upcoming campaign but getting upset over a lighthearted joke is an incredible waste of energy. It would also help if you had someone proofread your official comments. The following excerpt from your note does not qualify as a sentence as far as my understanding of English usage is concerned.

We and our children of this generation who have been educated and who have dreams of one day becoming the first African American president for all the people

I had the privilege of hearing Andrew Young speak back in the early '80's and I can promise you that he would never be caught dead releasing a public statement that is so poorly written. Take this sentence for example: John Kerry should apologize to every black child in America, children who have dreams, children who can succeed to hold the highest office in the United States as President.

You hurt your cause when you don't present your thoughts in a clear, proper, concise manner.

Phil

Ms. Harris,

Reading your words, simply makes me very proud to be your fellow citizen. I kept your comments to read again and to share with friends.

I applaud you for your reasons in organizing your business as a for-profit, rather than a non-profit adventure. I hope other people can and will see what a champion they have in you. Yours is the real leadership for truly changing the futures of an entire generation of kids. May God bless you in that business.

Beloved Citizen

Dear Ms. Harris,

You may rightly feel publicly indignant about John Kerry's ridiculous remark about being the "2nd Black President," but you owe it to Andrew Young and the millions of black youth growing up to equally denounce Al Sharpton using the word "Jew" as a verb, as in "they Jewed my message" in front of a public audience. The slur was recorded for all to hear, or ignore as the case may be.

This makes two for two black presidential candidates now (Jackson and Sharpton) who have publicly slandered the Jews on the campaign trail. No one seems to care, least of all black people. Is it because everyone hates the Jews? I doubt it. Or is it because black presidential candidates just don't warrant being taken seriously?

Regards,

Mayerson

I just wanted to offer my kudos to Paula Diane Harris for pointing out the hypocrisy of our "African American leaders" as it relates to some of our nation's politicians.

I believe that Senator John F. Kerry's comments, "President Clinton was often known as the first black president. I wouldn't be upset if I could earn the right to be the second." emphasizes what I believe is the Democratic Party's view as it relates to people of color: people of color can be in a position of power as long as the person's color is white!

I also think that the silence from our leaders in the "community" speaks volumes. Thanks for speaking up.

Curt

Ms. Paula Diane Harris:

Shame on you! Your attack against John Kerry is inappropriate and counterproductive. By launching a cheap attack against John Kerry, you give aid and comfort to George Bush and his cronies. Are you trying to ensure

George Bush's re-election?

Did Reverend Young sanction your words or are you just using his name to promote yourself at the expense of others? Are you making this attack to profit by hosting a debate? Your words bring dishonor to you, your organization and Rev. Young.

True leaders don't engage in cheap, counterproductive stunts. Think before you speak next time.

Greg

Bill Clinton thought of himself as "black" and mentioned it frequently. maybe John Kerry feels the same. If you all don't like it vote for Bush. He has your best interests in mind and always insists he is white…

Morgan, Cayucos CA

In this time of oppression by many sides I think it was inappropriate for your leader to take a small comment and turn it into an issue. Senator Kerry is not the problem George Bush is.

Wes

Jackson, MS

I have a question for Mc Paula Diane Harris in regards to her reaction to John Kerry's comments about being a "black president".

You say "Until you are born black in America and have walked in our shoes you will never earn the right as a white man to be called a black president." Poet Toni Morrison was the one who said that President Bill Clinton was America's first "black" president, meaning that he was the first President to actively work on issues pertinent to the African American community. Obviously, she was not saying that President Clinton was black.

Do you feel that Ms. Morrison's statement was unfounded? Do you think she was foolish to say so as an African American?

As a bi-racial woman, I am a bit confused by your reaction to Kerry's comment. Though he probably should not have said that out loud, the message that I got was that he hopes to be able to reach the African American community the way Clinton did. Let's hope he can live up to that, but not criticize him for saying so. Its time we got opinions out in the open, rather than hide them away.

Regards,

Laura

Paula Diane Harris
Washington, DC

"John Kerry is not a black man - he is a privileged white man who has no idea what it is in this country to be a poor white in this country, let alone a black man," says you. If you deny Kerry from equating with a black man, then you should deny yourself from any comment about any man - you're not a man. QED. PDQ.

You want social change; start by changing your constant race baiting. But, I guess you make more money by being a bigot.

There is only one race. Why don't you join?

Meyer

While it is admirable of you to express outrage at the ridiculous statements Sen. Kerry made, your position is sadly weakened by the infallible fact that come November the democratic candidate will be the one unanimously voted for by your members. Still this republican does sincerely appreciate the gesture

-Parjar

This is much ado about nothing!

More important to African Americans is that we learn to love one another. Stop doing all the bad things to our friends and neighbors and

154

others. We are our own worst enemy. I believe this complaint is baseless.

Another four years of Bush?

-Lucitay

Thanks for responding and I really do appreciate your comments - I did read your website before I had written my first email. I think that the message and its meaning and the candidate's desire to make that message come to fruition are the keys. Yes, all candidates need to earn all of our votes. It did seem to me that Kerry was actually trying to honor a past president who for the most part I believe did well for African Americans and the whole of the American people. It did not seem at all that he was implying that he was a black substitute - of course he could never be that. What he can do - I hope - is at least approach the black experience with understanding and perhaps wisdom.

So what prompted my email was that here is a candidate that at least seems to be making an effort - and his past voting record and other recent comments help bear that out - and then he gets blasted by your organization for a comment that meant he held this group dear.

Context is important. His overall message need not (and should not) change, but if he is in front of a Parent-Teacher Assoc or in front of a group of accountants, or in front of a group of veterans, his main discussion points naturally will be different.

In any case, in my opinion, the current administration is an abomination and needs to go.

Regards,

Andrew

Lay off Kerry. You are not helping. I now have radical right wingers quoting your organization as being against Kerry. You are not helping your constituency. An offhand comment is nothing compared to an entire platform built around further enriching the wealthy and keeping the poor right where they are. I think you should reconsider your comments, because they are being used by republicans to damage the democratic candidate.

Russell D. Abbott

Nichols

As a Black person I'm disappointed that this is the only pathetic manner in which you can draw attention to yourselves. You know what the man (Kerry) meant and to take it out of context in order to get some press just makes you look stupid. With so many pressing issues facing us as a people, i.e., lack of proper health care, jobs, education, and your public response was both disingenuous and trite. Why aren't you asking him where the 40,000 new troops he wants to send to Iraq coming from? Does that spell DRAFT and who goes first (poor minorities)? It's this kind of silliness that stirs up unnecessary confusion so when you really do have something to say no one's interested in listening. You owe your members an apology. Let's hope this was a ploy to get the candidates to notice you and debate but next time attaché a little intelligence to your plan and don't cut off your nose to spite your face. Hey but then again for all I know you're probably a Republican. In which case, never mind.

Barbara

Santa Monica, California

Hi Ms. Harris,

As a Black Man who has experienced racism, racist remarks, and has been a victim of a racially-motivated physical assault, I must tell you that I have ABSOLUTELY NO PROBLEM whatsoever with Mr. Kerry's "second Black President" remarks.

These remarks were OBVIOUSLY light hearted and meaningless, and-although I respect, and would be the FIRST to fight for, your right to Free Speech—I am at a loss as to why great minds such as yourself and/or Mr. Young would even waste your valuable time attempting to inflate such an issue when we have SO many other challenges (i.e.: war, poverty, REAL racism, voter fraud, etc) facing this great country of ours!

Many thanks to you and to Mr. Young for your past and future efforts to protect and to inform our community, and our nation!

Lamarr, Powder Springs, GA

I truly do not believe that the remarks Sen. Kerry made were meant to be offensive. I believe that he was stating that just as President Clinton was associated with the black citizens, he too would find it an honor to be so honored. I do not think he has to apologize, but rather carefully and clearly explain his comment. Let's face it, if someone wants to misconstrue the comment, then they will. That's sad. -Beejchris

---

Dear Ms Harris,

As a white, Republican woman I have often wondered if the reference to Bill Clinton as the first black President was designed to make African-Americans feel that they already have had a black man as President and could stop trying and expecting the Democrats to support one. It seemed like a made up story to make everyone in the black community happy with the Democratic Party. I hoped that no African-American was falling for this hype. For a while back a few years ago I even thought that the Republicans might just put the first black President into office.

I applaud what you said in your answer to John Kerry and his people to his wishes to possibly be the second black President. I especially applaud your many references to the fact that we need a person as President who will be for all our citizens. And I love your reference to all of us being members of the human race. I also think the world of politics is so much more interesting now that more and more African-Americans are venturing into and taking part in the conservative side.

Thanks for your thoughtful and concerned answer to the John Kerry campaign.

Sincerely, Caris

Question: If your organization supports the human race, and is trying to avoid race separation, then how come you don't speak out against media outlets like Black Entertainment Television (BET)? Don't you think that is racist? What would happen if white people created a channel called White Entertainment Television?

It seems to me that your mission statement contradicts your actions. If your group truly believed in unity, it would not support any races attempt to separate the people.

Anonymous

Paula Diane Harris:

I am distressed by your reaction to Senator Kerry's remarks which were clearly intended to be supportive of the African American community. Must the leaders of Black America take issue with every comment made regarding the interests of their constituencies without regard **to** the intent and historical context of such discussions? Perhaps it is difficult to pass up the chance at a sound bite or photo-op, but this commentary is unnecessary, in my opinion, and counter-productive. Slow news day?

Paula Diane Harris
Daniel

Boston

Hi Paula:

I am glad someone has stepped forward to address Senator John Kerry's ill-conceived remarks. They were, and are, offensive to most Americans. Sadly, they are emblematic of so many elite, affluent politicians — of the right or the left.

Thank you.

Rogers

Natick, MA

Dear Ms. Harris,

Thank you and your organization for speaking out on Sen. Kerry's ridiculous statement on "not being upset...BLACK President..." It seems appears that our "Black" representatives care not about what is said, but about who says it. Had a Republican made that statement, we would not have been able to get it off the airwaves, but because one our "kindly overseers" made it appears to be O.K.

Again thanks for speaking out on the statement, not the stator.

Eugene

As a black man from Africa leaving in this blessed Country, I am very often frustrated by our leaders who care more about their own interest than the interest of the community as a whole. We cannot blindly condemn republicans for their stances on social issues while we close our eyes to the same things done by democrats.

The comment by Sen. Kerry on becoming the second black President is not only offensive but it is a continuation of many politicians taking black votes for granted and saying anything to give the impression of them caring about the black community. Unfortunately, many of our brothers and sisters will fall for this type of comment and electing them into offices but in return, access will be given to the "leaders" and the rest of us will not see any improvement in the community.

-Tosh

Hahahahahaha. . . Andy, you sanctimonious twit! I get such a laugh out of you guys I can hardly digest my corn flakes! So John Kerry stirred up great righteous indignation within your reason-challenged club when he genuflected within tongue distance of your alligator wingtips begging to fill in for Pigville's favorite Bubba, and be nature's second black president 'eh? Hahahaha . . .

I imagine that had the Democratic party's darling-in-waiting, 'Mr. Ed' Kerry, had hinted he'd like to be known as a 'white' president, you'd all start foaming at the mouth, and between gasps of racism, racism, racism, begin boycotting Dryer's for marketing vanilla ice cream, Sherwin-Williams for it's white paint, Pampers for it's white diapers, and God, who, unfortunately is considered 'white,' for creating that bright 'white' moon we see smiling down at us on romantic summer nights.

It's not too often a rich, white, politician with grandiose illusions becomes comfortable groveling at the collard greens and back ribs trough - why not just sit back and enjoy it?

SM in CA

Hooray for you!

"John Kerry is not a black man - he is a privileged white man who has no idea what it is in this country to be a poor white in this country, let alone a black man," said Paula Diane Harris

- Randall

Paula Diane Harris Fantastic D and C article. Keep up the good work.

-Bratton

John Kerry really doesn't know about being poor!!

Thanks for telling him so - God bless you folks!!

-Phillip

Ms. Harris:

We've got major problems with an idiot in the White House, who is ruining our country, sending our youth off to die in a war that never should have been and turned his back on black America and held his arms out wide for the Confederate Flag flying, "Bubbas" on the NASCAR Circuit.

As an African American, I am getting sick and tired of our "so-called" leaders mouthing off without a semblance of concern as to the big picture. We don't need any sabotaging acts by self-important bit players like you. We've got an election to win and get a moron out of the White House. If you don't have enough executive savvy to know when and where to pick your battles, then your organization is in trouble.

What have you said about Marcus Dixon? Where is your outrage there? Not to mention where is your focus on the myriad of problems plaguing black teens, including killing each other like it was a sanctioned sport. Focus on the issues that are germane to your duties. Is Haiti a bit too deep of an issue for you to concern yourself with?

Don't try to become a new black spokesperson by showing a thin-skinned pettiness that should be beneath you. We are not interested in your opinion as to how offended you might have been about a remark that admittedly could have gone unsaid. It is always the intent of what was said that means something. Nonetheless, unless you convened your Board and got a vote to issue the press statement that you did, then you should have said nothing at all. Furthermore, if you have a Board, you should be down in front of the Governor's Mansion in Atlanta and yelling like "you know what" to get this young man, Marcus Dixon freed. I have sent $1000 to his legal defense fund. What has your organization sent?

We cannot have George W. Bush prevail in November. Think about the things that his Justice Department has done, DoD, Scalia, Thomas. Criticizing these zealots is a full time job. Leave Kerry alone, he is our only hope to gain some semblance of dignity and stature back in the international community and getting some sorely needed help fighting on the front lines of the streets in our cities.

Thank you,

John

Fairfield, CA

Blank Hello,

I agree with your statement that calling Clinton or Kerry the first
or second "Black President" is crazy and is extremely demeaning to the
African-American community. There are many qualified Americans of
African descent who could be great presidents given the chance. You are
correct to call Mr.. Kerry out on the carpet for that remark. I look forward
to the first "Real" black president.

Not some rich white guy claiming to be "black". Sounds like a load of
political horse pucky to me. Thank you for your time.

Regards,

Christian

Jackson Hole, Wyoming

Give me a fucking break guys. Kerry said that Clinton was often
considered the first "black president" by many Afro Americans and he
hopefully wanted to be the second. Clinton was called that by rap stars,
radio DJ's and various other black entertainers. Where were you then?
I guess it was ok because a "black man" said it right? Your know exactly
what context he was speaking in (Which both of us know is fine) and your
acting like someone just called your mom the "N" word… You are blowing
this way out of proportion and making a big deal out of nothing. You

guys really need to get a fucking life. I've seen black comedians on BET, HBO and various other cables and local stations that base their ENTIRE comedy routine making fun of white people for a laugh. And believe me, the comments they make are far more defamatory than this ridiculous sound byte you're making a mountain out of. You're setting a vicious double standard here just to get your goddamn name in the paper. Groups like yours shame the memory of prominent and positive black leaders like King… It's a shameless attack based on nothing, for nothing other than to further your own personal agenda. Get life losers… I can exercise my first amendment rights as well assholes…

-Magnacor

Bless you for standing up and telling it like it is. More to pity if this wealthy clown ever gets in the White House.

Yager

Thank you for your recent comments about Senator Kerry's ""2nd Black President" remark. I am not black but I too was disturbed by the senator's remark and am so very grateful for your speaking out about it. I wholeheartedly agree.

Sincerely,

Mitchell

Dear Ms. Harris,

just read your statement regarding John Kerry's asinine remarks last week. I want you to know that I am in full agreement with your response, which is something I've felt even when Bill Clinton used to make similar comments, but have not been able to articulate or encapsulate as well as you did yesterday. Statements like Mr. Kerry's are insulting to all Americans and show only how out-of-touch and patronizing privileged politicians like Mr. Kerry can be.

Thanks so much for speaking the truth even at the risk of political incorrectness or stinging rebuttals from our "leaders."

All the best,

Greg

YOU PEOPLE NEED TO GET OVER YOURSELVES. YES I SAID "YOU PEOPLE."

-Rick

To Whom It May Concern, I commend Ms. Harris on her comments regarding Sen. Kerry's remarks about being perceived as the "second black president..." Whether one agrees with Sen. Kerry's political agenda or not, I am heartened that Ms. Harris would take a stand and voice what many of us are thinking. Regards, Chas

---

Dear Miss. Harris:

I have no personal interest in this brouhaha. I couldn't care less about the color of the skin of the next president. With all the important issues in this presidential campaign regarding civil liberties, the environment, constitutional rights, the economy, national security, etc., you have latched on to something that is pure trivia. You know very well what Sen. Kerry was trying to say- that he would be proud to be known as an advocate for issues important to Blacks. He certainly owes no apology for that.

You have chosen to make an issue of it, I suppose to get your name in the press, garner your 15 minutes of fame and for your own political gain. I can only conclude that your organization is not one of substance. It's funny that your organization has never received this much publicity for anything else.

This is the meat of what is important to Blacks? This is not substance. Shame on you. Shame on you.

You'll get "social change" all right. But it certainly won't benefit your constituency. You'll probably get what you deserve, another term for President Bush. And that's bad for Blacks, Whites, Reds, Yellows and every other color.

Again, I certainly hope there are issues of real substance that interest you and other Blacks. If this is it, God help you. And don't blame others if your more important issues aren't taken seriously. This time you've alienated your potential political friends. Your political enemies must be having a good laugh!

Mark, Wynnewood PA

Mrs. Harris,

I understand what Kerry was trying to say and did not take it as an insult. Of course he doesn't know what it is to be black in America but if he can accomplish the type of things Clinton did the everyone will be making those comments/comparisons anyway. Frankly if he could fix the mess Bush created and accomplishes some of the things Clinton did I wouldn't care at all about that comment. I don't know what his record is but unless there is something more than that comment I'd rather allow his actions to speak for him not words.

Hopefully we'll get a chance to see what he's made of.

Just wanted to let you know,

Greg

As a conservative republican, I commend you for your statement, and agree with you, however, we came closer to having a black run for president last time, but he chose not to...I would have loved to vote for Colin Powell, a man of integrity.... M. Eiford

---

My family and I have willingly put ourselves in harm's way to try to help people of color in America. We have done this for over 200yrs. As our current spokesman I am telling you in no uncertain terms "knock off the crappy attacks on John Kerry".

-Emmitt

Dear Sirs & Mesdames,

I am always surprised that the original quote in its entirety by Toni Morrison isn't regarded as insulting.

Best,

Richard

San Francisco

Please try to limit your criticism of Senator Kerry to policy and not to an irrelevant social quib made on the campaign trail. What's truly disturbing is that groups such as you claim to defend the civil rights and dignity of Afro-Americans like myself yet fail to realize that the current administration is a bigger threat to our economic and social well being.

Please adjust your focus to the BIG PICTURE.

Desmond

Atlanta, GA

Thanks Paula!

No, Kerry isn't black, and Clinton wasn't either….

I applaud you for standing up for principle and demanding an apology.

It's about time!

Where were you when Clinton was declared the first "Black" president?

Where were you when Clinton violated the dignity of Women everywhere with his indecent and immoral sexual escapades?

John

Columbia, Tn.

You are right to criticize this comment by Kerry and to be offended. I am sure the major news networks will not speak of your displeasure, unless you stand up and request an interview with them about your viewpoint.

GOOD LUCK to you.

Gail in Texas

Please lighten up. Anger is easy. Temperance is difficult.

-Frank

Ms. Harris:

I saw your article linked from the Drudge Report and I had to comment. I don't have any personal background in the issues that you deal with in your organization, but I still very much appreciate what you stand for. I commend you for your thoughtful, insightful, and logical response to recent comments made by a Sen. Kerry. I appreciate that you stood up and said something. That is inspiring.

Thank you for your time and efforts.

Best regards.

Malachi, Colorado

I was glad to hear you commenting on that Kerry Black Pres. remark. As soon as I heard that I found it so offensive and even though I am white what difference does it make what color any of us are? We are all Americans and I thought to myself if I were black I would be even more offended-it just seems strongly like someone trying to affiliate himself for votes, which frankly it seemed to me Pres. Clinton sometimes did also. It's very easy for someone who has lived on easy street his or her whole life to talk lightly as if he could be black-talk is cheap. He will never be walking in those shoes.

-Linda

Congratulations on your response to Kerry's desire to be the 2nd Black president. It is truly an insult as was Clinton's claim. It's as if a Black person couldn't be his/her own 1st Black president. It's a patronizing lie and I am tired of the lies of the left. Your response shows integrity.

-Tom

Good Day,

I am writing you in support of your calling for an apology from Mr. Kerry, for statements he made the other day in regards to being "the second Black President". I find it insulting that he would imply that only "White, Blackmen" can become president. In these remarks, I feel that he is re-affirming the attitude in politics, that it is a white mans club. I also have a lot of trouble accepting that a man of his wealth and means can understand what it is like living from check to check. Men like Kerry and Edwards, howled like banshee's when President Bush, initiated the tax rebates. For me it showed that they have no concept of what $3,000 means to some people.

I am a disabled Viet Nam era Veteran, who's been fighting the VA, for going on 6 years now for what was promised upon enlistment. My financial problems are not the concern of any politician today. We are the forgotten Vet's. Oh we've been welcomed home, just don't try for any benefits. I can imagine that it is harder for a Black Veteran, than it is for me.

Sorry got off the subject. Point being, is he will say something along the lines of that isn't what he meant. I see though, that is exactly what he meant. The Democratic Party feels that they have the Black vote locked up and in their pocket. Yet they won't do anything more, than try to reward you for your support, by handing out checks. I just wish that Kerry and others would have to make a greater effort to win your vote, and then just taking it for granted.

If you read this, thank you and God bless you for the time you took,

Duncan

Ms. Harris, et al. should lighten up about Kerry's innocuous remark about being the second president for us. You are taking yourselves far too serious.

There are so many more issues that we as a people (and country) should concern ourselves. George Bush and his cronies have done, and are still doing, incalculable damage to this country. We must be determined to remove his administration from power.

We have seen what they are capable of thus far: lying, stealing, cheating, abusing the rights of citizens, etc. Do we really want four more years of that?

Please, let's stay focused on real issues.

I have checked your web site and am impressed with your work. Thank you.

Jim

Pinole, CA

Paula: You refer to the personal agendas of black leaders. That personal agenda is spelled M_O_N_E_Y. If they worked half as hard at getting kids through school and making sure those kids had a nurturing family consisting of a mother AND father to raise them things would get a lot better for black people. I grew up on a farm, dirt poor, never saw an indoor toilet until I was 12 years old, and graduated from a 200 student high school, worked and saved money and with my mothers help and father's encouragement and student loans graduated from college. I just retired at the age of 58 with a net worth of 10 million dollars. All the money in this world will not solve black problems. But with LEADERS like Jesse and AL the perpetual stereotype of the down trodden black who needs government help to succeed will live on, as will the resentment of those who have to pay the bills. How many more generations will be hood winked by the lies. Other ethnic groups come here and do beautifully. There are no Korean leaders, no Chinese leaders. What there is though is opportunity, work ethic, education, family values, and positive attitudes. That combination will get you there. I know, I'm living proof!!!! Pete

---

Dear Ms. Harris,

Thank you pointing out the hypocrisy of those who accept Mr. Kerry's remarks without reservation or concern. I believe you are doing the right thing. It is unfortunate that social and political organizations across the spectrum, left and right, fail to recognize their hypocrisy.

In my mind it only weakens their cause. For example, why didn't the National Organization of Women or other women's groups stand up against the exploitation of women when Janet Jackson was exposed on national television? I think it is because they didn't want to offend their freedom of speech friends on the left. They did a disservice to Ms. Jackson and their causes.

-Vince

Dear Ms. Harris,

I applaud your voice in speaking out against John Kerry's "2nd black president statement". I was shocked when I first heard of his comments. I remember thinking…when was the first? Your editorial was thoughtful and inclusive of ALL races, and further illuminates the racial divide the Democratic Party has been trying to manipulate. He should concentrate on earning votes rather than taking an ethic group's vote for granted. Thank you for speaking out when an outrageous political comment like that is made.

Sincerely,

Crowley

Hi,

I'm white and I grew up in the greater Boston area during the busing crisis. In the morning, we used to watch the protesters throwing rocks at busses and mobbing them, and then go off to school in our quiet little town with our paper sack lunches. I couldn't understand why people were so angry at the idea of sharing the nice schools with everybody and taking turns going to the schools that weren't so nice.

My husband is white too. He grew up in Murfreesboro, Tennessee. His high school was 50/50 white and black. He couldn't understand why everybody went to school together but went home to different neighborhoods and shopped at different stores.

I don't like how so many black men are in jail and on death row. I think whites get away with a lot more. I don't like the ugly assumptions made because of people's skin color or ethnicity. I worry that the new immigrants in my area (Maine) will feel discouraged after they figure out what is really going on in America.

I'm a peaceful woman, and my husband is a peaceful man. That's why I enjoyed your message so much.

-Barbara

To Paula Diane Harris,

While John Kerry's saying "I wouldn't be upset if I could earn the right to be the second [black president]" may not have been the most politically astute sentiment to pass his lips, your demanding for an apology may constitute an even more egregious pandering for attention. He said that he hopes to "earn the right," which rebuts your claim that he takes the black vote for granted. Your complaints may do damage to the causes you hope to uphold—many of which, incidentally, are shared both by John Kerry and me. Sincerely,

Grant

You CEO's remarks attacking Kerry were the most stupid I have heard from a person of color in fifty years! If your organization stands for anything it must stand for a color-blind society and anything that aids and comforts enemies of social justice contradicts that conviction. The Bush-Cheney gang has done more to harm equal opportunity than the KKK in recent years.

For your information, it was some of our most respected Black Leaders that affectionately gave the title of "first Black President" to Bill Clinton. As a person of color, I say shame on Mrs. Harris and her compulsion to join the Vichy crowd.

-Hank

Paula Diane Harris,

I was pleasantly surprised to read your comments regarding John Kerry's desire to be know as the second black president, However, I hope your remarks won't be misconstrued as an attempt to censure the senator's right to pander. Please prepare yourself for the inevitable forthcoming criticism along the lines of "how dare you question John Kerry's patriotism, er... blackness, er... whatever."

Best regards,

Bill

P.S. were you aware that John Kerry served in Vietnam????

This statement just made me so sick that I decided to return to my roots and change my party affiliation. If I can't have Andrew Young as my president then it sure as hell will not be Kerry. He is a fraud and a fake. When my granddaddy went to register to vote the Democrats turned his black face away, so he became a Republican where they welcomed him. But for some reason, my parents and embraced the Democratic Party believing that they were "our" people. I have had it now. Kerry is a bigot in sheep's clothing and I am no longer a Democrat. Why are we not getting behind

Sharpton?

-C.M.

As a White boy born, raised and educated in Georgia I appreciate your comments regarding Kerry. You are right in looking at being used and abused by the Liberal Democrats.

Maybe when we look at each other as Americans with something to offer each other as individuals we will throw off the yoke of Political control by a minority of party members. I am not happy with the Democrats or Republican Party.

As to qualify African Americans to run as President, I would love to see Colin Powell sitting in the chair myself. I appreciate what he has accomplished in his life. I would rather see his hand on the nuclear button than Dick Chenney's.

-Charles

Hello,

I am so happy about your criticism of John Kerry comment about wanting to be the second black president. When I heard him make the comment, I thought it was in poor taste and was an insult to African Americans all over this country. Thank you for speaking out on this subject.

Gary

I agree that John Kerry totally insulted Black Americans by asking to be the next Black President. He is a white man of privilege. Maybe there will be a real Black President someday. And by the way how about his vice president?

The Democrats have the black vote tied up so why bother?

Pam J

Chicago

Just my two cents worth: I also thought the comments were stupid for Kerry to say. I too was shocked to read about Kerry wanting to be "the second black president." However, right now we really need to focus on getting rid of Bush. Kerry might not be great, but he heads and shoulders above Bush that is for sure. Instead of focusing on those things, which divide democrats and all others who wish to see Bush leave office, we should be concentrating on what pulls us together. Let's get rid of George W. and then we can focus on the stupid things politicians say.

Ben

Please pass along my sincere thank you for Paula Diane Harris' demanding an apology from John Kerry regarding his statement about wanting to be the second black President. It is good to see a black leader unafraid to come out against what most of us are thinking rather than acquiescing to their personal agendas.

Sincerely, Dante

To Paula Diane Harris,

John Kerry was trying to be complementary and appeal to the Blacks and you have to try and make it a racial issue…. You people are never satisfied…why don't you just lighten up.

Bob….Ft Worth, TX

The Real first Black President will be a Republican. The first real black Vice President will be a Republican. The first Real Black Secretary of state IS a Republican. The Second Supreme Court Justice is a black man and hated by all who consider themselves people of color. The first was half African American half White.

The current Vice President of the US has a lesbian daughter, the

conservative black Supreme Court Justice has a White wife, and Jeb Bush is married to a Mexican and all of his children are mixed race and his son will run for President as the first Mixed Raced Presidential Candidate. The democrats are the Diversity Party. Riggght?????

J. C Watts is out of the scene for now but soon he will reappear as the Republican Nominee in 08 and you all will have to make the hard decision to turn your back on another Great man coming from your society. Your first Black President is White Trash and the Second is Rich gold-digger.

-Steve

American Justice Dot Com agrees with Ms. Harris' statement regarding John Kerry. Such remarks by Mr. Kerry wanting to be the '2nd black president' are disingenuous to say the least. It would be all the better if he were humble and sincere.

Sincerely,

Terry

American Justice

To Paula Diane Harris:

What business have you got insisting on a Kerry apology? So naively letting yourself be set up to foster the filthy Bush campaign. You are ignorant and obviously, willingly or not, a simple patsy for the right wing millionaires destroying real democracy. You do not deserve the name Andrew Young connected with yours. It is obvious why you do not make it easy to be e-mailed. You should resign now, because if you are not a plant, you certainly are naive (or sinister) enough to be one.

-Michael

Paula Diane Harris

To: Diane Harris

As much as you criticize John Kerry's comments referencing Clinton and being the "2nd black President", your method of reaction and overly sensitive nature, without regard for the intent and context in which it was intended is more obnoxious and nitpicking than any criticism of Kerry and his comment that I can think of would warrant.

While Kerry's choice of words may have not been the most "politically correct" his intent was clear, and instead of jumping on his words, you should be embracing his real message and intent. It's people like you who just look for things like this to criticize (which could have easily been done more effectively in a private letter to his campaign) that I personally find more insulting to blacks than Kerry's actual comment. You should find something productive to say before you mouth off —-we'd all be better off in that case!!

-b.h.r.y.

I think that you people are always speaking just so that b/s you say can be heard! What is wrong with Mr. Kerry wanting to be the next Bill Clinton? Bill was a great man. So just shut your damn mouth and vote for Mr. Kerry when the time comes! BUT THE WAY YOU SOUND YOU MUST BE A BUSH LOVER————BECAUSE AFTER THAT B/S YOU PUT ON LINE AND IN THE PAPERS YOU SOUND LIKE A SUCKER TO ME!

FROM: A BLACK MAN-WILBERT

Does Ms. Harris really believe her motto: There's only one race-the human race? Then why did she take such pains to point out that Mr. Kerry does not belong to the African American race? That demand for an apology is one of the silliest issues I can imagine any serious civil rights group taking up. Comments like that will insure that you are never taken seriously-at least by me.

Did Ms. Harris object when Toni Morrison called Bill Clinton the first black President? No. Because it was and still is considered a compliment. Why, then is it a bad thing for John Kerry to wish to consider so favorably by blacks?

-Melba

A NON- ISSUE...........and there are some great ones out there.

-Alice

I believe a Black writer, Toni Morrison, used the term "The First Black

President" to describe Bill Clinton. So please tell me what is the problem with this term being used for another person that might be a President that all Minorities would be aided by him being in office. Thank You.

Troy, Ohio

I want to thank Paula Harris for getting it right. Kerry is no black man. Neither am I, but his remarks offended me. I wonder when the black community will realize that the Dems have done nothing, absolutely nothing to improve the conditions in the black community. I don't get it.

-Tracy

The political world can't be so bereft of intellect that people don't recognize pandering for the insulting behavior that it is. So it's a really sad statement that you are the **only** person I've noticed with the intellectual honesty to call John Kerry on this particularly ugly remark. Thanks.

—— Robin

I wanted to say that I thought Ms. Paula Diane Harris showed a lot of courage and leadership when she rightly pointed out how some in the Democratic Party are using African Americans, to further their own political agendas. I thought her comments about Senator John Kerry were well said. I am proud of her willingness to demand accountability in our leaders.

Bill, Texas

I think your public remarks criticizing Kerry is outrageously self-defeating. Kerry would do far, far more than Bush to help the poor and people of color if elected. You should consider the consequences before you speak. Any public criticism of Kerry benefits Bush. If Bush is elected, the lives of African American's will only get worse.

Also, you completely misunderstood his remarks, possibly intentionally. You know what he meant: He meant he wants to be so supportive of Blacks that you'd think he was Black. Obviously, he and Bush are both privileged Whites, but only Kerry has the voting record that proves his commitment to helping the poor and victims of discrimination.

Martin, PHD

Bless you ma'm. You are one of the very few that see what the Democratic Party and its candidate are all about. Promises, promises, promise, but no cigar.

-Sid

I find it refreshing that you are not letting Kerry get away with his racially offensive comments. There is no way this man will ever know what it is like to be a black man and to suggest that he would be a "black" president is insulting to every African American young man that aspires to the highest office in our land. Keep up the good work. Don't let him get away with these self-serving comments.

Dawn

"John Kerry is not a black man— he is a privileged white man who has no idea what it is in this country to be a poor white in this country, let alone a black man." The point is that Kerry is much more likely to be concerned about and willing to do something to positively effect the situation of minorities in America then is George W. Bush.

That you would ask for an apology is odd. If Kerry is able to help improve the lives of Americans, including African Americans it will be because he tried. He will have earned what he seeks. Please, lighten up.

-Mark

It is obvious that Kerry is more of a good president for the Black people than Bush. Bush is loaded with broken promises galore. We need to unite behind Kerry instead of casting doubts. Bush will be the end of anything that could help us. He wants to create a nation of two classes, the rich and the poor!

-Ramon, New Mexico

Hello,

I would like to thank you for demanding that Senator Kerry apologize for his ridiculous and demeaning remark made recently about wanting to be the second black President. His absurdity in assuming that blacks in this country would want a white man acting as their "black president" is indicative of a lack of resonance with the black population.

Sincerely,

Kiera

Dear Ms. Harris:

Try lightening up a bit. Getting angry at the drop of a pin is a sure-fired way to induce hypertension in oneself.

Was it one of the brightest things that came out of John Kerry's mouth? No, of course not. In the spectrum of things to make one angry at on a scale of 1 to 10, with 10 being the most likely, this rates a 0.5. Get over it. We've got bigger fish to fry, namely George W. Bush.

Sincerely,

George, IL

Ms. Harris: I am a life-long Republican — but, the fact that Mr. Kerry of multi-million dollar homes, Forbes family background would deign to be the "second Black president" is very galling. Having been raised in a very, poor white family and having worshiped with black people at a time when I did not understand why Bro. Bird would not stay and partake of a luncheon — I am saddened and disgusted when I hear a Mr. Kerry use people for his own agenda. He is very insensitive. I like your quote — "There's only one race and that is the Human Race" —

Regards,

Doris

Dear Ms. Harris,

Thank you for your statement about Mr. Kerry's remarks about being known as the second "Black President". It is time our politicians stop using "race" in a Political agenda and began promoting responsible citizenship by offering all people a chance to become a part of the American Dream. I invite you to come to Mississippi to let us show you many examples of "success stories" We are not a nation of "RACE" but of ideals and liberty and we need to remind our Political leaders of America's uniqueness in the world.

Thank you again,

Norman

Mississippi

Understand you may feel that Kerry is an overpriveledged white male, and therefore hardly representative of most African Americans, you might want to consider the big picture before you go Kerry bashing as he attempts to campaign against George Bush. Kerry is not African American, but is far more progressive than Bush, who you may be helping. I think it is quite obvious Kerry was not speaking literally when he said he would like to be the next black president, and while I would welcome a black president myself, there simply isn't going to be one this election cycle. Kerry "I'd like to be the next black President" still certainly beats George "I have no problem with black people—I think everyone should own a couple" Bush.

I can promise you, there are other places I will be sending my financial support to rather than your organization in the future, if you wish to remain so bitterly entrenched. You seem to want to cut your own nose to spite your face—do it with your own cash.

Mark

Oh come on. You totally misrepresented the spirit of John Kerry's remarks. If you are just looking for attention, you should be ashamed. The one who is now owed an apology is John Kerry. John Kerry and his party are the most influential friends African Americans have in Washington. Instead of taking political potshots at them in an effort to publicize your company, you ought to be working hard to make sure they get elected. Some people can't see the forest for the trees. I know one company that I would never get involved with. Shame on you.

-Brad

Paula Diane Harris

Dear Ms. Harris,

This comment is particularly offensive to me when it is remembered
that Clinton was called the 1st black president, as I understand it, because
of his trouble with the law and because he grew up in a trailer park with
a single mother. Perhaps, Mr. Kerry should clarify what he means by his
comment. This link shows where the comment was first made about former
President Clinton.

I agree with you that the black vote should be earned by the democrats.
They have promised much for a long time, but have not delivered.

I wish you the best with your organization's quest to help others.

cw

Dear Ms. Harris,

I read your comments in reply to Mr. Kerry statement (wanting to be
the second Black President) - I just want to say - THANK-YOU!

You see, I am a white woman - I may judge people based on their
personalities, abilities etc. but I always see the differences, the uniqueness in
each of us. Saying that one does not see something to me is to ignore and
not validate another. I believe that those that say they "don't see color" are
those that very much looking at the differences. I say - see the differences
and embrace and applaud them. This is what makes us unique, human, the

person we are.

Kennedy was the first Catholic president - as yet we have not had a black president - and I have often been upset by the claim the Clinton made that he was. No he wasn't. Unlike you, I do believe in our lifetime there will be a president of color. I know there are people that are very bright, capable and would and could offer a lot to this country and will one day run for president. This person may very well be a Republican and not a Democrat. Time will tell.

I do agree that candidates should earn votes- votes from all people. I agree no one should assume and expect that because they are there that we owe them a vote.

I wish more people heard your remarks- I think it would be eye opening for those that are taking citizens for granted. I also agree that those that run for president are president for ALL of the people - we are not a separate group but a whole nation.

Thank-you,

Connie

Dear Ms Harris:

John Kerry's recent remark about wanting the honor of being the "second black president" was indeed very insulting—-and it is not my intention to apologize for it. You were correct in calling attention to such a remark; I think your comments will actually help Senator Kerry 'get ahead" of such thoughtless attitudes. He always struck me as a man who is being continuously educated and trying to be a better person.

I first heard of John Kerry when he appeared before a Senate committee in 1970 to address the many concerns of Vietnam veterans. His statements and the manner in which he handled himself helped me deal with my own thoughts about having served in Vietnam and helped me to do what was necessary to *finally* get over it. I do not believe John Kerry is a saint, but in a contest against George W. Bush I have no doubt about which man stands for the for the right things in America.

It is up to you to decide which of these men will best serve African Americans.

Sincerely,

Gene

Jacksonburg, West Virginia

You're not actually trying to help Bush are you? Please! Think, perhaps about Kerry's comments!

Geller

I don't see many blacks qualified for the White House. But there are some. Check out the Republican Party. The blacks that are on the Democratic Party are considerably less delectable, not because they are black but maybe because they spend a lot of time talking about how bad white people are. What you are accusing whites of it doing what you are now doing. Making wide accusations about a race of people. You are insinuating that most, if not all, that most, if not all, whites are spending their days trying to oppress black people. I would NOT vote for anyone who speaks that way about me, would you?

We do agree on this- Kerry is trying to put the minimum amount of oil on the African American Voting Machinery. Everybody knows that it is obligatory to sit in a black church, grin like an idiot, and pretend that you feel quite at home among the black congregation. Privilege is just the word. Kerry is as far from understanding poor people (that's me by the way) OR blacks. He is just hustling you to get your vote. But isn't that what your black leaders do too, isn't it?

Rick

Sir/Madam:

I am an African, now an African American. I am very highly educated and highly informed politically. I have contributed significantly to Black causes including working to make Historical Black University competitive in Research and development with mainstream Universities.

I read your note about Kerry whom I did not support much during the primary with dismay and I take issue with you. I think Bill Clinton was better President for Black people here and world wide than any Black American would ever have been. If precedence is anything to go by, look at what you have to Today - Clearance Thomas he hates whom is, he lacks identity, and hates Black people, Collin Powell and his son, total disaster, - Collin Powell did not want to go into Liberia to save them when everybody even Liberians wanted Americans, but he sold the invasion of Iraq in the United Nation when Iraqis did not want to be rescued, he did not attend the Conference in South Africa on slavery, he helped dethrone Aristide, first of by cutting off funding to the impoverish country, then blaming him for doing nothing. Look at Rodney Paige whom I know personally. He makes a fool of himself daily, his stupidity speaks for itself. I just mentioned these men because they are the highest-ranking Black men in this Administration. I am very proud to be African American but I dislike Black men that are scared to be whom they are. Blacks. They sell out to white people until they are in trouble and then people like you will try to protect these losers.

I don't want to paint everyone with the same brush, but your statement about Kerry was childish and immature and played into the Right Wing's hand. I am disappointed that such statement was made under the banner of an honorable man like Andrew Young. So-called black leaders (name only) stink so much that in our primary here in Houston, in my district Al Green (black) is running against Chris Bell (white). I am having a problem deciding whom to vote for. My heart says for Al but my mind says Chris

Bell because African American Leaders wants to out white whites when they get a little power so why don't I just vote a white person.

Kerry's statement is on the money and you guys should not fall into the trap set for you by the Right Wing. You already have in away because you just made the same statement Matt Drudge made, shame on whoever brought this idea up. You are distracting Kerry and Democrats from going after these racists in the office. God Bless you. - Diego

---

Why are you making such an issue of Kerry's remark about being the second black president? He was trying to identify his values with those of the black race.

Me thinks that you are a Republican patsy is disguise.

God help us

Oliver

Ms. Harris,

I thought your rebuke to John Kerry was much needed and well done. Thanks you!

I am a lawyer in Florida. If I can help your work, please let me know.

-Jack.-

Dear Ms. Harris:

Thank you for putting into text exactly what many people must also have on their minds regarding Mr. Kerry's comments on being the next black President. I find his comment to be offensive not just to African Americans (I know this after reading your comments and discussing it w/ friends of mine) but it seems offensive to all educated, thinking people, regardless of skin color. As your average, middle class white guy, I am insulted that Kerry tries to portray himself as anything but a privileged person from an upper class white family. It's not just a matter of race, but also one of socioeconomic status. That he feels the entirety of the populace can be so easily duped is quite presumptuous.

As for your comments regarding having a black President in the White House: Heck, most people will vote for the man or woman who they feel is most qualified for the job. I believe strongly that we have black Presidents in our future and women as well. May we both be around when the time comes that a person's qualifications is all that matters. Good luck in your continuing endeavors.

Respectfully,

Steven

To whom it may concern…

I think your comment on Kerry's statement about wanting to follow in Clinton's footsteps is childish and detrimental to all of us. I am not a Democrat or a Republican, I am neither rich nor poor, and am of different racial genetics. For someone who usually stands for the good of the people, tearing our one hope down in this bipolar two party system will do nothing but hinder our chances of kicking the worst president in the history of mankind out of office.

-Snowy

With all due respect (and from one African American to another), one would think that an organization such as yours would have something better to do than to perceive insults where there are none. Perhaps you're so busy with 'social change' that you haven't time for common social experiences like … use of humor to make a point! Senator Kerry's remark was — to everyone in the world but you — a lighthearted acknowledgement of the sympathy that most African Americans feel from and for President Clinton and an admirable — in my estimation — expression of Senator Kerry's desire to enjoy that same kind of special relationship during his own presidency. One can hardly imagine how any rational (or not otherwise motivated) African American could be offended by that. Then again, that begs the question, doesn't it?

Be well … soon.

Kenneth

As a white man partially raised in Atlanta by a wonderful black woman, a hippy with long hair in the South in the 60's so I very much know what it is to be chased and beaten by rednecks, a music business executive in the South with many long, late honest nights shared with black artists, and, finally, someone who clearly and proudly remembers standing in the front of the crowd on Auburn Ave as Dr King's mule-pulled funeral caisson rolled by (were YOU there?), I am ashamed of you.

If you only knew what the fake-smile Republican wasps really say around the backyard Bar-B-Q as I can (until I've had enough and just leave), you would NEVER NEVER be stupid enough to give the republicans ANY ammunition like you did with your picky little criticism of the Democratic candidate. WHOEVER HE IS!

Trust me. If you believe that John Kerry (or any white person) cannot have real knowledge of the lives of people of color, then I will honor your view. Generally, this is true. However then, you cannot know the real feelings that the close-minded, old south Bush supporters express in their own company.

I do and they are still ignorant and I don't like it. Take it as gospel that you will be doing a bad thing for your people and all people if you encourage the right wing again with silly and weakening opinions that the republicans can use to try and keep power. Power that they will use - maybe they just don't know any better, who cares - against the people they do not see as equal.

Help us bring enlightenment …don't hurt our effort anymore please. Praise the Democratic candidate.

Thank you.

To: Paula Diane Harris

I was frankly amazed at your response to Senator Kerry's remarks on the Urban Radio Network. Very seldom do I see well-respected organizations twist a meaning to its most perverse level. To draw the inferences you did, I must assume you seek to divide, not unite. Your choice of calling Mr. Kerry "Privileged" seeks to stereotype any white man as being somehow undeserved of praise or honor. I am sure that when Sen. Kerry was wounded in the service of our country he did not consider himself privileged. Is it your wish to taint everyone not **born** into poverty? To quote an old favorite: "No rich man shall every know the depths of neither my sorrow, nor I his troubles". You can never walk in anyone's shoes, or be them; you can only be the person you are.

Mr. Kerry cited that President Clinton was known as the 'first black President'. This being an obvious metaphorical reference to Clinton's efforts on behalf of all people, especially African Americans. It was not Senator Kerry who gave him this moniker. It was Toni Morrison. You may know who she is, if not, it is your loss.

Senator Kerry did not say he WAS black, or that he knew what it was like to be black. Here merely said (paraphrased) that he would be honored if he could fit into Bill Clinton's shoes with respect to "all-inclusiveness that seek to span races and preferences:" Sounds like a noble goal to me. Do you disagree? Is it your position that he should not take an aggressive stance on these issues? Perhaps he should follow G.W. Bush's lead on this?

I guess the part that caused me the greatest worry is the fuel your comments have given those who are definitely not on the side of any rights, except for those of extreme privilege. You have given them the ammo they need to continuously chip away at our rights.

Perhaps you should apologize.

Dave

San Diego, CA

Hey Paula! Get a grip.

-Hector

Paula, do you really think that Kerry was asking to be seen as "black"? Don't you think he might have been hoping to be seen in the same light (super positive, for good reason) among Blacks, the way Clinton was? Did you object to this characterization of Clinton? Are you a shill for the RNC? Don't you think there is enough hate and contention without you helping to keep us in the gutter is such a knee-jerk manner? dk

David, California

Thank you for speaking out against Mr. Kerry's comments. I do not understand why people accepted the comments about Mr. Clinton, and it is time that these race-baiting comments stop. I feel like Mr. Kerry is just trying to get my sympathies. I don't even know who to vote for anymore.

Well, keep up the offensive on him and those who are like him, and I'll do my part here in Houston.

Have a blessed day,

-Jeremy

I read this evening of your reaction to Senator Kerry's comments and I really think you are jumping to conclusions. If it had truly been racist in intent then he should be taken to task, but that was NOT the point of his comment. His voting record in the Senate surely indicates he would be a great president for all Americans.

Please think carefully about how close this election will be and what is needed to turn President Bush out of office. Every time there is infighting among Democrats or Liberals the Republican Party can barely contain their glee. When you consider issuing press statements on such a trivial issue you further the re-election cause of George W. Bush.

If you think this is a cause really worth fighting for and perhaps cannot pick the largest dragons you want to slay, reconsider. If you think the major issue is principle, keep in mind that Ralph Nader is of exactly the same mindset when it comes to his campaign for the presidency.

Hoping for a Democratic victory in November,

Christopher

Get over yourself Paula. As a black Texas Democrat — strongly opposed to Bush or any Republican being re-elected — I am incensed that you choose to pick a fight with John Kerry over semantics. In my lifetime, Clinton was about as close as it comes to a black president — and if Kerry wants to follow in his footsteps we should applaud him. Organizations like yours obviously take themselves too seriously. I am absolutely sickened to read about your displaced anger, and can only hope that the rest of the country will find your wrath nauseating also.

Brian

Austin TX

Granted Ms. Harris, Bill Clinton obviously wasn't the 1st black president so no way can j Kerry, of all people, be the second. You realize it was a Toni Morrison line he referenced, of course. But as jokes go both were pretty mild considering they were meant to be ironic rather than hilariously funny. If anything they chided Americans for the very thing you talk about in your article: that so far the white house is for whites only and that it's wrong. I so wish there was a decent candidate in this election but there isn't. Speaking only for myself, Kerry is far from ideal and bush is even farther. To me, bush has done a surprising amount of damage in less than one term and I'm really bummed by the thought of him getting a second one. So, not knowing how or even whether, you plan to vote this year, I'm wondering if your intent was to give bush some help. Reason? I found your article from a top link on drudge report, which has been leading with 'Bush is great/Kerry is evil' stories since Super Tuesday. Frankly I think Nader, Dean or Sharpton would be better for the country but at this point it's just bush or Kerry. Unfortunately, yes. Anyway, just letting you know that I read your article and you're absolutely right. Idiotic remark. Kerry's no jay leno for sure! However, Kerry has a very long way to go before catching up with bush on gaffes. Remember, "Africa is a nation that suffers from incredible disease." Whether helping bush win reelection is gonna make the day come any sooner when a real black American becomes president is another discussion, but I don't think it will. Please take a look at yahoo's message boards sometime and see how some pro bush people are crowing about your remarks. If you think those people will ever allow a black American to serve as president, pls check them out on the other news story message boards where they spew racism and curse the poor almost every time they post. Libs are demonized constantly for tolerating diversity, although it is expressed in the crudest terms imaginable. They say things like "you should all be shot", and I wonder if they're crazy enough to really mean it. Just for saying unemployment's a problem, for example. Not very nice people!

Peace,

q

Would you rather have bush/Cheney in charge for 4 more years, or a John Kerry who actually gives a shit about those of us getting screwed by the almighty republican aristocracy? Gary, Green Bay, Wi.

" President Clinton was often known as the first black president," Kerry told the American Urban Radio Network. "I wouldn't be upset if I could earn the right to be the second".

It is sad that candidates will say anything for a vote. "I consider John Kerry's statement regarding his earning the right to be known as the second black president an insult," stated Paula Diane Harris, Founder, President and & CEO of the Andrew Young National Center for Social Change Inc. John Kerry is not a black man— he is a privileged white man who has no idea what it is in this country to be a poor white in this country, let alone a black man. Civil Rights leaders in this nation sit back and ignore these types of comments, a practice that further insults African Americans. It seems that all these leaders care about is their personal agendas in how a "John Kerry" will keep up their personal causes. They forget about the issues that affect our people, especially our young people, who are struggling every single day to obtain an equal, quality public education.

Kerry's comment is another example of the mentality of some members of the Democrat Party who take black votes for granted. It is time our votes were earned. This election is too important for ALL Americans to have time for this type of theatrical statement. To the candidates, I say, "Stick to the issues that affect ALL Americans and run on your voting record and the issues. Stop trying to single out one minority group in this country for their votes. If you want black votes, EARN THEM by sticking to the issues in what you as president are going to do if you are elected."

Kerry's comment is another example of the mentality of some members of the Democrat Party who take black votes for granted. It is time our votes were earned.

"America today needs a president for ALL the people. It is time we began to look at people not by their race but by their citizenship as

Americans. There is only one race and that is the human race", stated

Paula Diane Harris.

-Marcus

I mean it is entirely up to the CSCI to request an apology from anyone they choose. But I fail to see the insult in what John Kerry was trying to convey in his remark about aspiring to being known as the "second black president". Clinton was instrumental in bringing jobs and prosperity to the African - American community. For John Kerry to aspire to do the same for blacks is a positive.

While you're asking for apologies, please consider asking Bush to apologize for his tacky gesture at one of his million dollar fundraising dinners in CA last week. When introducing a fellow African American, Mr.

Bush then proceeded to rub his head. Which I understand is an old-time belief that rubbing the head of an African American brings good luck.

Mr. Kerry will make a better president for African American's vs. George Bush. If you care about African American's, which I'm sure, you to, then it's in the best interest of poor & middle class whites, blacks & Hispanics, to support Sen. Kerry. Bush has proven himself as a man who only supports those with money and corporate donors.

As a Hispanic woman, who grew up in the projects - I want an apology from Mr. Bush for lying about Iraq, under funding No Child Left Behind, giving more importance and money to RX & insurance companies vs. Medicare recipients, trashing the environment, and stonewalling the 911 investigation.

I was always told to choose my battles carefully. In the case of you're insisting on an apology from Sen. Kerry for his light-hearted remark - is misguided.

Terri

Ms. Harris,

Your comment regarding John Kerry is out of line.

It is ridiculous for you to criticize Kerry's desire to be held in the same regard as President Clinton.

John Kerry is apparently aware of all of the Blacks Clinton appointed to Cabinet-level positions. Mike Espy, Alexis Herman and of course the late Ron Brown. Franklin Raines - the current CEO of Fannie Mae - served as Clinton's budget director. Clinton appointed J. Terry Edmonds as the White House's first Black speechwriter.

For John Kerry to recognize these actions should inspire your support as an African-American, not your baseless criticism.

John Kerry may be a "privileged white man." But isn't it at least one goal of the civil rights movement to have people "who have no idea what it is in this country to be poor and white in this country, let alone a black man…" to reach out and try to understand? And to ask "how can I help to improve things for Blacks and poor Whites?"

It seems liked Kerry was inspired by the generation that included the man who your center was named after, Andrew Young. It seems like Young and his contemporaries inspired Kerry to ask himself what he can do to help. And here you are, slapping his hand away for no reason.

For the record, I am African American. For the record, I have nothing to do with the Kerry campaign at any level.

Ms. Harris, no candidate is perfect. As we both know, even President Clinton had his warts. But George W. Bush appoints the ultra-conservative Charles Pickering as a U.S. district judge to sit on the 5th U.S. Circuit Court of Appeals during a Congressional recess and Kerry says he would like to be held in the same regard as Bill Clinton by Blacks… And You Decide to Pick A Fight with KERRY???!!!!

I think you need to step back and take a good look at the big picture.

A real good look.

Regards,

Osok

Hello, I appreciated your position on Senator Kerry's statement and was surprised to find that you are local. Although by now I'm guessing you know that, you are linked on Drudge Report. I think that the pandering that occurs on all sides is misleading and offensive, and you certainly made that perspective known. I read over your website, and further appreciated the manner in which you approached the issues of racial equality in general, and especially your emphasis on the need for social change.

In any case, I appreciated your opinion, and I applaud the volume that your message has garnered.

Respectfully, Treff

To Whom It May Concern:

I just read an internet story regarding Senator Kerry's comment and Ms. Harris' response. As one who studies African American politics and Race and ethnic relations, I was appalled at Ms. Harris' criticism of the Senator's comment about wanting to be known as the second black president. Does Ms. Allen know what a metaphor is? This kind of attention seeking, self-serving criticism does nothing to improve the condition of the people that the National Center for Social Change claims to represent. Perhaps Ms. Harris should take note of her own words and her organization's motto: "there is only one race, and that is the human race." If she believes this, why is she so conscious of Senator Kerry's race in her comments? It seems to me that Kerry's comment is completely consistent with the sentiment of transcending race.

Kerry

My gosh, give it a rest. Kerry was trying to be a friend. Why start a war with a friend?

If anyone needs to apologize, it is you to Kerry for attacking him so needlessly.

Can anyone spell "heal?"

-DPG

As the head of a law firm in Philadelphia that fought racial discrimination in individual cases and class actions starting in 1972, I find Ms. Harris' remarks about Kerry's statements to be ignorant grandstanding, and calculated to elect Bush, a true enemy of civil rights (and the advancement of ordinary blacks) by virtue of his judicial appointments alone, to say nothing about his other policies that are just as damaging, if not as overt.

Kerry, speaking metaphorically, was promising to be so sensitive to the issues of blacks that the race would symbolically adopt him. What more could any group expect from a candidate. Moreover, there are issues that affect blacks that are not shared by others, and it is the converse of taking blacks for granted when Kerry addresses black issues specifically instead of ignoring blacks, as Ms. Harris prescribes. Furthermore, while Kerry's record seems quite friendly to blacks (e.g., which candidate is opposed to the death penalty—and which race has historically had more innocent people executed?), but one's record is the past, and we are voting for what the candidate has learned and promises to do in the future based on his experience.

Any fool can attract a crowd and attention. But considering the options in 2004, Ms. Harris has demonstrated not just a lack of sensitivity to the results of her gratuitous outburst, but a failure to even understand the rather obvious meaning of Kerry's statement. Ms. Harris made the big time when the Drudge Report picked up her mindless statement. While advancing Ms. Harris' own agenda, and perhaps earning favor from the Bush team, she did potential harm to the philosophy espoused and lived by Andrew Young.

Surely Andrew Young was never happy with the right wing Supreme Court that cut down the life-enriching gains made by ordinary people as a result of the rulings and wisdom of the Warren Court. If Ms. Harris helps Bush win, the result will be a century of anti-people rulings from right wing, elitist judges who favor the government business and bigots as opposed to the average guy. This leads to the conclusion that either Ms. Harris is the wrong person to be speaking on behalf of Andrew Young's philosophy, or that the organization is a fraud in using Andrew Young's name.

Gary

Philadelphia

Ms. Harris,

Thank you,

I have felt for a long time now that we have been patronized by the Democrats and I am sick of it. As much as I hate to say it. And my family would just die to hear me say it. Bush says it like it is. And his actions speak volumes. FCC Chairman, Sec. State. NSA and much, much, more. In my book he is not the divider.

J.

Dear Sir/Madam,

Without being necessarily a supporter of John Kerry, I am incensed by the requested apology for the recent remark made by him about not minding to be the "second black president".

Perhaps we could all make a step forward by ceasing the apparent practice of referring to "African - Americans" or other terms of similar nature. This is, with respect, a racist term, and by accepting all citizens of whatever color, race or creed as "Americans", we might actually take a step forward to removing, if not eliminating, discrimination.

Very truly yours,

J W

Miss Harris:

Thank you for finally (someone from the Black community) stepping up and lambasting these patronizing Democrats for their pompous attitudes towards you and most Americans. You hit the nail when you stated," It's about time these candidates EARNED our votes instead of taking us for granted!" How many times have I shouted that same thing at the radio and at the television set! The Black Americans have for too long been asleep when casting their votes for the Democrats. Clinton did NOTHING to earn the title. I was ashamed that he even repeated that patronizing, stupid lie…. but he did and a lot of folks believed him! And what's with that Harlem office??? (That is what the Dems do…repeat a lie enough and then folks believe it…and take it as fact. Once that happens…it is very nearly impossible to disprove it.)

I will be very happy to vote for the first Black president when he steps forward and if he fits the qualifications that I look for in a president. I have a prediction: The first Black president will come from the ranks of the conservative side of the aisle…and he will be a Christian! Also…he will be anti-abortion, anti-gay 'marriage', moderate who has a grip on reality. He will have arrived at his position thru extreme hard work…. with out handouts! He will also be a great speaker…able to motivate and move people with his intelligence and grasp of the issues that face America during his watch. He will also be fearless in the face of the terror we face in this new world.

We have the best golfer…and I mean we, even tho I'm white, in Tiger Woods. We had the best basketball player…Mr. Jordan. The best tennis players in women…. Williams sisters. The best trumpet player in Wyntin Marsailles (sp). Some of the best actors in Hollywood…and the list goes on. There is NO reason we can't have a black president…none. But I think it will only happen when Black America wakes up to the fact that the Democratic party in not doing them one bit of good! Black America is only being used by them. Look at the people Clinton had around him…. now compare that to the Bush Administration. It is self-evident. A Bush-Rice ticket in '04 would be the perfect ticket and Kerry and his patronizing minions wouldn' stand a chance!

PS> Hillary is the most dangerous Democrat out there. She has only one desire…. power and to be the first black/women president!

Thank you for taking your stand…. and I'm going to put your web site in my favorites list.

Jim

Bloomington, Mn.

Ms. Harris,

Thank you for your strong statement in regard to John Kerry's desire to be the 2nd Black President. Not only is it an insult, it is also a transparent attempt to garner votes from African-Americans. In many ways, it is bigotry in its rawest sense. For him to believe that he could ingratiate himself to the Black voter in this manner indicates his lack of understanding of the issues facing not only African-Americans, but all Americans. He is out of touch. I do hope George Bush and John Kerry accept your invitation to debate.

Sincerely,

A.J.

It's about time I heard a Democrat called out by an African-American organization on such a pandering comment as the one made by presidential hopeful John Kerry. I had gotten to the point where I really came to believe that the American Black population was incapable of having an original thought. The Democratic Party has been pulling the wool over the Black populace's eyes for way too long in this country. Leave partisan politics behind and let's all open up our eyes and work for the good of a country for everybody

Thank you,

Jim

Congratulations on your insight on the Democratic Party.

This is a party that has, for years, taken the black vote without ever really doing anything at all for black people. They toss African Americans a hate crimes law and a little affirmative action and expect blacks to fall in line and put up big numbers for them at the polls every fourth November.

But what have any of them really done besides visiting your churches and clapping along to the songs that they never seem to know the words of? It's funny, but most of these politicians never really seem to know blacks even exist until election time comes around. Even then, they visit your churches, pretend that they're going through the same thing you are (check Kerry's comments at a black church in Jackson, MS this past weekend), clap through a few songs, and then disappear knowing that you're going to vote for them anyway because they've convinced you that Republicans are a bunch of rich-boy church-burners.

Paula Diane Harris

The Democratic Party is the new plantation. John Kerry logic says, "If I can make you dependent on me via affirmative action and welfare, you'll have no choice but to keep me in power or take a chance on seeing your livelihoods disappear. If I can convince you that my government programs are the only way for you to survive, that need for survival will keep you voting me into office.

It's sick, but it's reality. And African Americans are allowing it to happen.

-Stick

I WAS GLAD TO SEE THAT SOMEONE FROM THE BLACK COMMUNITY STEPPED UP AND

RESPONDED TO MR. KERRY'S REMARKS ABOUT BEING THE SECOND BLACK PRESIDENT. IT WAS PANDERING TO THE EXTREME. IF HE TRULY CARED ABOUT THE BLACK COMMUNITY, HE SHOULD HAVE SAID, "HE IS LOOKING FORWARD TO THE DAY THAT THERE IS A BLACK PRESIDENT."

PLEASE DON'T GET TAKEN IN AGAIN WITH RHETORIC. ANYONE CAN SAY ANYTHING, BUT YOU MUST ASK YOURSELF "WHAT DO THEY DO WHEN THEY ARE IN OFFICE?" I BELIEVE BLACKS HAVE THE INTELLIGENCE, AND STRENGTH TO BE WHATEVER THEY WANT TO BE TODAY.

YOU DON'T "NEED" TO LEAN ON ANYONE. I SO LOOK
FORWARD TO THE DAY WHEN YOU TELL THEM "ALL" TO GO
TO HELL AND START TAKING YOUR RIGHTFUL PLACE IN
SOCIETY.

YOU HAVE A GOOD START WITH CONDI RICE, AND
COLON POWELL. (They are wonderful)

KEEP UP THE GOOD WORK AND DON'T LET THEM GET
AWAY WITH ANYTHING!

JOAN

Fear not people, Kerry wont be the second Black President not even
a white president, They love him so much down here, Turnout for the
Primary is predicted to be less than 10% and in ST.Landry parish about
maybe 5% Har de Har,Har

-Nick

Dear Ms. Harris:

Did you read/hear the entire sentence Kerry spoke? Why don't you just
admit you didn't get it, you took it way too literally, and you're attacking
the wrong guy? Attack Antonin Scalia, attack Dick Cheney, attack James
Dobson of Focus on the Family — these people are right-wing NUTS and
you're attacking the best hope this country has to _survive_ after 2004?

Come on, now. We have a right to free speech, not dumb speech. I'm talking about you, not him. Don't yell "fire" in a crowded cinema, and don't give the right-wing Republicans another peg to hang their deranged presidential campaign on. Okay? Thanks.

Scott

Ann Arbor, MI

Condoleezza —Black-female-intelligent, AND Republican—Condoleezza…From black in the south to the nearest so far-black in the white house… Let Kerry choose MADAME Hillary as his running mate vs. Condoleezza as Bush VP and let the chips fall….Condoleezza for PRESIDENT in 2008!!!!! What say you???? From a Hispanic Republican for the USA!!!

-Barney

Thank you to Diane Harris for saying what she did about John Kerry, he has no business and neither did Bill Clinton, saying they are black, I am a white male 53 years old living in Canada and neither one of them I am sure has any idea the struggle and hardships that the black population of the U.S.A. has had to endure for may hundreds of years. I sure wish more black leaders would speak out more often about this pandering that goes on, the democrats have been saying for 50 years, you black folk vote for us and we will change everything for you all, well it hasn't changed and they would just love to keep the blacks in the country beholding to them so they have power over you all, Ms. Harris you are a smart lady and I hope you voice is heard loud and clear in the black community.

cya… Philip… :-)

Ms Harris,

Your statement of fact is awesome. One day we shall have no barrier to any qualified leader stepping up to any office of our great country.

Eddie

Dear Paula Diane Harris:

At a time when African-Americans- like those living in poverty and on through to the middle class- are suffering from the policies of this current administration, I would think the idea of getting into the political fray for a media opportunity is something that serves the one and does not benefit the many. We as African Americans- including members of the Congressional Black Caucus- have called Clinton the country's first black president; a moniker that demonstrates how much criticism a candidate, were they black, would have to endure regarding sexual activities, policies, etc.

Considering the assault by the Bush Administration on African Americans, I would think you'd find compelling reasons for more of our people to get out and vote in numbers that would make El Fondren proud (remember him, a former slave who voted for the first time in Lowndes

County during the turbulent civil rights campaign). Instead you focus on the minute and not keeping your eye firmly focused on the prize. What a shame. And shame on you.

-Stavros

Poor silly Paula. It was Chris Rock who said that Clinton was the first black president. Not some rich white man. And he said it because Clinton was sympathetic to black issues and because he was being treated as if he was black, what with the investigations, the impeachments, and the intrusions into his private life.

All Kerry was trying to say was that he too wanted to be especially responsive to black needs. That is what he meant and you know it. And you have a problem with this?

It appears that all Paula wants is publicity. She should try to do so by DOING SOMETHING positive, not by making silly comments like this.

HOW MUCH DO YOU WANT TO BET THAT BILL O'REILLY WILL BE BEGGING PAULA TO GO ON HIS SHOW AND CARRY HIS WATER FOR HIM? AND WHAT DO YOU WANT TO PUT DOWN THAT SHE ACCEPTS?

-Leo

My wife and I appreciate your stand against the misrepresentation by Bill Clinton as the "first black president" and the added insult by Senator Kerry to be "the second black president".

Keep telling it like it should be. We are color blind, but our ears are a burning over these gross misreprentations and a slap against African Americans.

Housers

Dallas, Texas

Ms. Harris,

Kudos for speaking out about John Kerry's insensitive comments. Too often, when politicians make statements like this, their racial pandering is overlooked.

Best regards,

Mark

God Bless, you Paula for your comments re Senator Kerry. At last a voice of reason and telling it like it is!!

Mrs. A.

Columbus, Ohio

Just read your response to Mr. Kerry. Why don't more Blacks / African Americans speak out like this more often? Call out the politicians and the self-appointed "Leaders of the Black Community" on this and other issues!!!!!!!! What you say is true!

-Martin

Dear Paula Harris,

Sen. Kerry's remark seemed strange to me. I hope he thinks about how he says things this year. I think he is a good man, even though he's disconnected by wealth and whiteness. I think, for white guys, Kerry and Kennedy (both rich) have worked hard on civil rights.

To clarify something, I'm no politico. I'm a carpenter from California, and I've worked across the country from here to Oregon to Georgia to Hilo.

I have a good perspective of racism from many angles, because I have seen its forms everywhere I've gone. I've been kicked out of a black town for being white and out of a white town for being a hippie from California (Atlanta suburbs) I've heard the car door locks snap down as I use a crosswalk. I've seen riots where men, black on white and white on black, kill each other in front of my eyes.

On the other hand, I've yet to know a person of color that did not like me; although I've never understood that. Except that, any engravings of racism I may have received in my life were reversed by the words of Dr. King and the Kennedy's in the '60s. Unfortunately, it reversed for only some of us; but that is why the Andrew Young Center exists.

In the quest for equal rights, be positive, be inventive, creative and steadfast, and avoid friendly fire loses. 'United We Stand-Divided We Fall' is the perfect motto for everything America should stand for and attempt together to dispel the division of racism and class. The politics of division can destroy decades (centuries) of progress.

Please give Sen. Kerry another chance. I think he means well. He just needs to speak well, and add "civil rights" to the "economy" and "the war" in his platform.

Thanks for listening Jeren

I second your thoughts and comments on your webpage regarding the 'second' black presidency. Hopefully someday a truly qualified African American candidate—regardless of party affiliation—will run for the highest office…. and win.

Good luck to you

Jim

Paula Diane Harris

Dear Paula:

How I hate to write this.

There is no Black American that can support Clinton's claim to be the first Black president. That was an insult to every Black American, and is just an indication of the pandering that white politicians will stoop to in order to hustle the Black vote.

We let it slide, but Clinton was as rotten and corrupt as politicians get. Kerry is not as bad as Clinton, but he certainly has little in common with Black America! He wants the Black vote, sho nuff' but he is every bit as rotten as the rest of the Massachusetts liberals that come to the south to hustle the darkies.

I just hate to see the pandering honkies hustling the Black vote. We deserve better and need to demand better. We also need to realize when we are played for ignorant fools by arrogant politicians.Best Wishes,

Lamar, Beaverton OR

Ms. Harris:

Congratulations! I think it's about time that someone in the black community expressed concern at the pandering of politicians. Not a one has followed through on any of their promises, but, instead, forget all about the minorities they condescend to until the next election cycle.

All they really say in their speeches is that your people are dumb and gullible. And they are proven correct at each and every election. People who find themselves in hopeless positions can't be blamed for looking for a light, however, and the politicians exploit this.

Charlie

Agree

N.W. Washington DC

From Republicans everywhere, THANK YOU!!! Why would Kerry apologize to you anyway, your not a black man either. But you are in the papers aren't you? So who's got the agenda?

-Vincent

Please doesn't let john Kerry use this "black president" business to advance his agenda? He's a rich white man with a rich white wife…shame on him!!!!

C.D.

Paula Diane Harris. Some people will take advantage of everything they can… You were right in asking for an apology

-George

Dear Ms. Harris,

I read your comment about Senator Kerry's remark being a second president to black people. He has no idea about poor blacks and many other people who are poor. You nailed him. He will not represent blacks now or later. He will use them for his own ambition.

I am white. I grew up in the inner city of New York years ago. I trust Colin Powell and Condo Rice and other prominent blacks that are bright and decent humans. If God were a black God, I would still pray and devote myself to him/her. It does not matter, God loves all humans. These evil politicians have an agenda. Democratic politicians are evil people. I would not have any of them as a relative or parent. I had some great black friends in the Army way back in 1957-59. All these years I think of them from time to time.

Thank you again Ms. Harris for speaking out against Kerry. He is not a man who believes in God. He is not honest. He called Vietnam veterans both black, Latino, white as war criminals. He has discredited their honor and courage.

Keep up your work.

Love

Frank

Do presidential candidates from the Democratic Party ever visit white protestant churches in the South when they are campaigning? Thank you.

C.K.

Chapter III
Courting the Black Vote

The definition of courting is **a man's courting of a woman; seeking the affections of a woman (usually with the hope of marriage); "it was a brief and intense courtship.** Do you remember how it felt to be courted by a gentlemen suitor? Some would call it wine and dine a person until they got the ultimate prize whatever it was they were after. You know how it goes; a man will tell you he loves you, wants to take care of you everything you possibly would want to hear. He plants the seed of security the suitor never knowing if he will follow through. It's an undertone of a promise that he will take care of you. I am so glad I did not raise my daughter with these expectations from men. I raised her to develop herself taking advantage of opportunities and education so that she could count on herself in being her own independent provider.

The Democrat Party was very smooth. It planted a seed of security to the African Americans in this country through dependent federal and state programs making them more and more dependent. They nurtured them supporting affirmation action knowing for the most part that the average African American did not benefit from affirmative action, the white female did, their wives and daughters benefited for the most part.

They have approved of civil rights organizations such as the NAACP to become an extended family member only to use the organization to mobilize black votes to support white democrat politicians. Many black elected officials run in primarily black districts and that is why you don't see as many County, U.S. Senate, U.S. Congress elected officials and governors that are African American. The vote territory becomes larger and blacks' become the minority vote.

In addition, the type of African American candidate who may run in a primarily black city area would not necessarily be able to cross the color line to attract white voters in higher elected offices. The experience and education for an elected official should no longer be taken for granted. People years ago that did not finish high school would not think of running for an elected position. But today, you can be elected even if you can't speak the English language. Education and experience no longer gets you elected it is money. Unfortunately, money has no education requirement or expectations.

If a white mayor for instance wants to stay in power in a primarily black community for 30 years with no term limits all they have to do is run their own team of African American candidates using their own financial resources to get their team elected. The pay off is I get you elected and finance your campaign you vote my way and never vote in term limits! An all black city council can give the appearance that they are black but in reality they sold themselves to the master. They are owned and bought and belong to the white mayor. This is very typical in how black Americans allow themselves to be used and placed in bondage on what I label a political slave plantation. For most of them it's the most they have ever had in their life. It makes them feel accepted and powerful. They actually feel they have succeeded. Remember I gave you the definition of courting - it all relates.

How does in this example the major's power grow? The answer is they use the Jim Crow techniques. Blacks who are considered house slaves are planted in organizations to become their ears and eyes. Their assignments are to disrupt the mission and leadership only to eventually destroy the organization leaving it voiceless. Because African Americans are so very content and passive and do not protect their civil organizations they become an easy target for take-over leaving a socially disadvantaged community defenseless.

Even though today black Americans no longer just occupy the inner city areas there aren't enough in suburban and in rural areas for them to elect themselves outside of most city governments. This is why the first African American president must be able to attract white voters and white financial backers in order to have a chance to win and clinch a major political party's nomination.

In this country we desperately need political reforms. It is time that the socially disadvantaged groups in America came together as one with our issues, demanding a seat at America's table of decision. Taking our votes out of the major parties by registering as an independent voter will make politicians take our issues seriously and will make them earn our votes and not take them for granted.

Black American votes are being taken for granted by the Democrat Party. It is felt by many African American's that their issues are not considered in the Republican Party. Has anyone from the African American sector including the National Black caucus leadership actually sat down and spoke with the current leadership of the Republican National Committee Ed Gillespie to discuss our concerns? Or is the perception of the Republican Party as NAACP Chairman Julian Bond described Republicans when he stated to hundreds of cheering liberal activists, singling out Republicans as enemies of Black Americans comparing conservatives to the terrorist Taliban who once ruled Afghanistan.

The statement in my opinion from Mr. Bond is racist and does not represent the mainstream of black America. His statement has shown how through the leadership of the NAACP has lost its focus and purpose. I am sure that the NAACP accepts money from Republicans for their cause. The NAACP's memberships alone is made up of Republicans (Black and white), Democrats, Independents, all ethnic groups in America, not counting the numerous white owned corporations that donate huge suns of money to the NAACP that helps pay those large salaries at the national and regional offices.

The NAACP is a non-profit 501c3 and has numerous 501c4 local branches across the United States. It is supposed to be non-partisan.

In any argument there are two sides and I contacted the Republican National Committee with specific questions. Regarding the RNC workforce they stated they are pleased with the diversity of its workforce. I would like to share the questions and their responses.

1. What did the RNC Chair think about the statement from John Kerry when he stated" He wouldn't mind earning the right to become the second black president"?

Response: Surprised.

2. Currently, African Americans are the most loyal voter group in the Democrat Party. Regarding the RNC what do you think are the major political differences between the RNC and the DNC?

Response: The Republican Party was born as the party of Abraham Lincoln and today we continue to be dedicated to the ideals of freedom and equality for all. President George W. Bush optimism, inclusion and pro-growth policies are empowering all Americans, including people of color. The result of these policies is that 35% of African Americans between the ages of 18-25 no longer consider themselves Democrats, but Independents and they are more willing to look at the Republican Party. 43% of African Americans believe the Democratic Party has taken them for granted.

Black Americans support President Bush's pro-growth agenda, from parents who support No Child Left Behind education initiatives, to first time homebuyers and small business owners.

Business incentives and tax cuts, by the Bush administration and Republicans in Congress, have helped to jump start many of these businesses, as a result, the number of small businesses launched by minorities is growing fast – up 17% annually, according to Fortune Magazine. Another recent survey on entrepreneurship found that African Americans are 50% more likely to start a small business, than the population as a whole.

For most minorities, home ownership is the key to obtaining the American dream. Under President Bush, that dream is becoming a reality; with minority home ownership now at an all time high. Over half of all minorities now own their own homes. The President's Americans dream down payment act, signed into law in 2003, will help 40,000 families a year, with down payment and closing costs.

The No Child Left behind Act improves our public schools, and we're seeing positive results with test scores up. This is important to the African Americans community, where only 12% of 8th graders are proficient in reading, 7% in math. We must end the soft bigotry of low expectation by having accountability in our schools. This president has provided an unprecedented amount of funding for education (49%) since he first took office.

Nationally, the black American unemployment rate dropped a half percentage point in April from March's 10.2% to 9.7%.

3. What is the RNC looking for in taking a candidate running for the presidency serious?

Response: At the RNC, we work hard to elect the Republican nominee for President. Republicans from the state house to the courthouse.

4. Does the RNC have an outreach program to recruit minority race individuals within the party" If so, explain the programs:

Response: The RNC has launched an unprecedented grassroots effort to grow our Party by reaching out to all constituencies across the ethnic, religious, and ideological spectrum. We have a Team Leader program designed to reach out to specialty groups and build grassroots activism. Team Leaders consist of various constituency groups. We're proud of the more than 1 million Team Leaders who are working aggressively in communities all across the nation to educate and activate their neighbors. Our African Americans Team Leaders are among over 36 team leader groups we work with, every day, in communities across the nation. In addition, this past June, Chairman Ed Gillespie kicked off the RNC's "African American Economic Empowerment Tour", with boxing promoter Don King, Miss America 2003 Erika Harold, Maryland Lt. Governor Michael Steele and Texas Railroad Commissioner Michael Williams.

Making stops in Detroit, Philadelphia, Cleveland, New York, Miami, and the tour is designed to talk with African American business owners about President George Bush's economic policies. The Chairman has also reached out to pastors, educators, parents and Historically Black College and University presidents.

Ed Gillespie, Chairman of the Republican National Committee stated that "Under the leadership of President Bush, the Republican Party is committed more than ever to including new faces and new voices in our Party- and the Republican Party is working toward a record level of support from Black voters this election".

Gillespie further stated "It is not in my interest as the Republican National Committee Chairman that 90% of African American voters vote Democrat election after election. More importantly, more and more African American voters are realizing that it's also not in their interest. Black voters deserve a two party system too!"

This is why it is so important to get the facts and not go by racial statements that were made by Julian Bond Chairman of the NAACP in making your decision. This is why Martin Luther King Jr. was so successful in his leadership because he was able to communicate with people before just labeling them as the enemy. Martin Luther King Jr. and the civil rights movement and all the people behind the movement were focused on the issues that affected people's lives regardless of their political affiliation. If you think that there are no prejudices democrats think again.

We must keep the doors open and be able to communicate effectively with people. It is time to learn that it is all right to disagree but wrong to be disagreeable. Research to find the facts, stay focused on the issue, not focused on destroying the messenger just because you disagree. Yelling and screaming calling people names only further shuts reasonable people down not taking your cause serious. There are no winners when this occurs.

It is time that political candidates, regardless of their party affiliation, are made to earn the votes. Registering millions of voters in one party prior to an election only allows them to take our votes for granted. It is time to get smarter; to register independent. We need to make the major parties earn our votes and we need to change the voting laws in states where independents cannot vote in primaries!

The United States Constitution begins with "We the People…NOT we the major political parties! Key Voter Political Reforms that need to be considered are:

Same Day Voter Registration

Voters should be able to register on the same day (SDVR) of an election, helping to increase participation — especially among young voters who on a high majority are on college campuses and need to change their voting location. The standard for verification is higher than other forms of registration since one has to provide ID on the spot and proof of residency. Voter turnout in the U.S. is among the lowest in the world. Only 34% of the eligible electorate came to the polls in the 1998 elections. The national average of 36% voter turnout ranks the United States at the bottom of all Western democracies. Voter turnout, for instance, among New York's youngest voters has hit an all-time low — less than 17% in recent elections. Compare this to states with SDVR where voter turnout has increased participation by upwards of 25%. Minnesota, one of only six states with SDVR, led the nation in 1998 with 60% voter turnout to elect independent Jesse Ventura Governor. Nearly 16% of Minnesotans who voted registered on Election Day, half of them were people under the age of 25.

Term Limits

this is a powerful tool against Democratic and Republican party incumbency. It would, for instance, limit the terms of Senators and Assembly Members to between 6 and 8 years. It brings an end to life-long career politicians, and allows for citizen-run rather than special interest-run legislatures. It has been supported at levels of up to 70% in elections throughout the 1990s. Term limits are also important in our city and local government elected positions such as mayor, city councils and county offices.

Ballot Access

Reforming access to ballot is crucial for greater political participation of eligible voters and candidates in the U.S. For instance, to run for President as an independent candidate for the first time, one needs to gather up to 40 times more signatures that either of the major parties. The ballot access laws should be rewritten to facilitate rather than discourage candidates from running. Petitioning periods need to be lengthened to make it easier for insurgent candidates and independents to qualify for a place on the ballot. Voters should be permitted to sign as many candidate petitions as they desire, and anyone should be able to circulate a petition. One-third of the states do not impose restrictions on who can circulate. However, in states like New York, candidates' families, supporters and friends cannot help them petition if they happen to live in a different district. So, while minor party candidates for statewide office in New York must collect the signatures of 5% of their enrolled voters, Democrats and Republicans need less than .05%. This requirement makes statewide petitioning virtually impossible for minor party candidates. In addition, voting is a right not a privilege. People have paid the ultimate sacrifice for the right to vote. It is discriminatory for some states to not allow an independent voter to vote in the primaries just because they are not affiliated with a political party.

Initiative & Referenda

Twenty-three states permit citizens to circumvent their legislatures by circulating a petition ("initiative") to place a proposed legislation ("referendum") on the ballot. New York is one of the many states without I&R. The fist step toward I&R would be an amendment to the New York State Constitution. The State Legislature could pass a Constitutional Amendment, but it is unlikely that the bipartisan controlled Legislature would be willing to do this since it would mean jeopardizing their steady flow of special-interest dollars. The alternative is to pass a Constitutional Amendment at a Constitutional Convention. That there will not be one until the year 2017 is an indication of how stifled democracy is in New York.

Non-Partisan Municipal Elections

This eliminates party primaries and increases both participation of candidates and voters, who are exposed to broader range of choices. Major cities, such as Los Angeles and Chicago, already have this reform in place.

In fact, over 80% of municipalities in the country with populations of 200,000 or more elect their officials through non-partisan elections. By removing party primaries, non-partisan elections give voters a broader choice of candidates from whom to choose. Non-partisan elections also allow for more meaningful public debate and increase the possibility for innovative policy solutions. Non-partisan elections would also change the character of the legislature for the better, since legislators would be less concerned with crossing their party for fear of retribution if they sought to run for reelection. Finally, non-partisan elections would help foster new citywide coalitions, which would serve to unify cities - not pit groups against each other. Non-partisan elections would therefore offer more options and greater power to voters to decide on policy-making decisions. Expert testimony given to the Charter Revision Commission in New York by Dr. Allan Lichtman, Chairman of the History Department at American University, points to the fallacy of the attacks by those who claim that non-partisan elections discriminate against minority voters. He cites a National League of Cities survey that found that in forty cities with populations of 50,000 or more with elected black mayors, twenty-nine were elected through non-partisan elections. Legislation is also needed to restructure local Boards of Elections to include minor parties and independents, functioning as non-partisan agencies.

Campaign Finance Reform

Campaign finance reform measures are needed that would level the playing field between independents and the majors. One way to do this is to tie the acceptance of public financing of campaigns to an agreement by the candidates to participate in public debates. Americans should be allowed to direct their own tax dollars to support the development of independent parties. New York City, for instance, has one of the most innovative and successful campaign finance programs in the country. It is a matching fund program, which outlaws corporate contributions and includes an agreement by the candidates to participate in publicly televised debates. It should be adopted by the whole state.

Open and Inclusive Debates

Public debates afford voters an opportunity to learn about their candidates in ways that campaign literature, television ads, radio commercials, and the internet do not. The pseudo-governmental bipartisan Commission on Presidential Debates should be abolished in favor of a non-partisan body that sets equitable criteria for the inclusion of candidates at the presidential level. Local non-partisan bodies should also serve to facilitate debates.

More and more career politicians try and weasel their way out of debates. One of the worst inventions is a candidate forum. These forums allow the candidates to not answer questions from the public and it allows them not to run on their political records. Instead at a candidate forum they tell the public what they want them to hear not what they need to hear. They pass out their literature and that's it folks!

Debates are crucial in an election and public service elected officials work for the people and they need to again answer to the people not to who just funds their campaigns. We hire elected officials at the polls and this is where we need to fire them! California proved that "We The People" have the power not the elected officials when we use the power of our democracy voice at the polls when they fired Gray Davis (D) former California governor and hired Arnold Schwarzenegger (R) in the recall.

2004 Presidential Campaign

The Democrat National Committee (DNC) targets the African American vote and reminds them constantly how the Republican administration has made them suffer numerous setbacks that include:

- Unemployment almost doubled the national average.
- 700,000 more African Americans living in poverty now than under President Clinton.
- An increase of the number of uninsured African Americans.
- President Bush's attack on affirmative action that resulted in a case before the Supreme Court.
- The nomination of ultra-conservative judges who will turn the clock back on civil, worker and woman's rights—including a recess appointment of Charles Pickering, who requested a lenient sentence for a convicted cross burner.
- The under funding of President Bush's own education initiative by $8 billion, forcing schools to cut back on programs, teachers, and supplies.

Why do the Democrat's target Blacks?? One major reason

Is because they need to court African Americans in order to win elections. Over 92% of African Americans are registered as Democrats. Democrats have become a controlling lover of the Black population the kind that is jealous and thinks they own you. The taking for granted is getting worst and my advice is to get a restraining order. Now I realize that it takes two to fight in any argument or problem so African Americans do have to take some of the blame for this suffocating love affair with the Democrats.

Let's begin with education. Education must become a priority in every African American home. Families must be partners with their children and the teachers that educate your children. The schools can't raise and shouldn't raise your children spending more time with discipline problems then teaching.

I support every word Bill Cosby had to say what I don't understand as reported by the media is why the **NAACP leaders were stunned by remarks of prominent comedian. It is time that those who have influence in the African American village stood up and told them the truth. Children "at risk" are big business and the jails such as in the state of Pennsylvania are being built for your children not more schools. .**

Bill Cosby made his remarks at a Constitution Hall event in Washington DC night commemorating the 50th anniversary of the Brown versus the

Board of Education decision that paved the way for integrated schools.

In the presence of NAACP President Kweisi Mfume and other Black leaders, comedian Bill Cosby took aim at blacks that don't take responsibility for their economic status, blame police for incarcerations and teach their kids poor speaking habits.

Black leaders evidently accepted the statement Kerry made because not one of them stood up against it. However, when a black tries to tell each other the truth they are ridiculed by other blacks. This is exactly why our civil rights organizations have lost credibility because they do not stand on principal. Instead they stand on being the oldest and the largest but what about being the most effective? Being large and old without character, purpose and strength doesn't equate to being efficient or valuable.

Department of Education currently administers a budget of about $63 billion per year and operates programs that touch on every area and level of education. The Department's elementary and secondary programs annually serve approximately 14,000 school districts and nearly 54 million students attending more than 93,000 public schools and 27,000 private schools. Department programs also provide grant, loan, and work-study assistance to over 9.5 million postsecondary students.

How can people say that not enough money goes into public education? How can the argument be made that the No Child Left Behind Program is not funded? Money is not the problem in public education. The problem is how those funds are being allocated within the school districts. There is no "watch dog" over the funding to ensure the funds are going in the classrooms not on the football field or basketball courts.

As an example, in Harrisburg Pennsylvania, the public school district is one of 12 districts on the states empowerment list since it was developed. The Harrisburg School District is approximately a 98% African American public school. This school district was by legislation taken away from an all black school district and placed under the control of the white mayor who was given the power to choose his own empowerment team made up of black and white house slaves. During this period several African American educators were released from their positions. Under the mayors control a "white" football coach was hired for $87,000.00 dollars for one school year. Numerous documents were sent by me, the previous president of the local NAACP branch asking Mfume to come to Pennsylvania to meet with these educators and discuss the litigations regarding taking the school district away from the all black school board and the firing of several African American educators but the NAACP from the national office never came. Finally, I got a meeting with Mfume to come to Baltimore to the national office to discuss the education situation in Harrisburg. The day before the meeting was to take place the national office called and cancelled the meeting never to reschedule.

In the year of 2000 the Department of Education of the Commonwealth of Pennsylvania, under the authority contained in Act 16 of 2000, the Education Empowerment Act, as amended by Act 91 of 2000, named numerous school districts, Harrisburg (approximately 98% African American) being one as on the Education Empowerment List.

The percentages showed the percent of students in bottom group of the PSSA scores in 2000 a two-year average for the Harrisburg School District, Dauphin County. Their percentage was 66.7% of their students scored in the bottom group. This is the same school district under the mayor leadership that a football coach was hired for $87,000.00 for one year. The problem is not if enough funds go into public education but rather how those funds are allocated and utilized within the school districts. The "No Child Left Behind" which is a good concept should give high standards for school districts to meet academically. The school districts need to make the appropriate cuts in their budgets to ensure academics in the classroom are the priority. Budget limits for athletics such as hiring coaches for $87,000.00 need to be but in place by local school boards. Food programs and after school day care programs need budget constraints because these types of programs should be the responsibility of the parents. You shouldn't buy a new car when the old car runs fine and the roof is falling in. It's all about setting the right priorities.

The Department of Education currently administers a budget of about $63 billion per year and operates programs that touch on every area and level of education. The Department's elementary and secondary programs annually serve approximately 14,000 school districts and nearly 54 million students attending more than 93,000 public schools and 27,000 private schools. Department programs also provide grant, loan, and work-study assistance to over 9.5 million postsecondary students.

Instead of fighting for more funding in education we need to be advocating for validated state standardized tests along with a fair academic measurement of classroom instruction for all students. We need to cease in making taxpayers pay for programs that are the parents' responsibility for their children. Each school district needs qualified teachers.

Philadelphia Pennsylvania for example, students aren't the only ones struggling to pass tests. Half of the district's middle school teachers who took tests to become certified as highly qualified under the federal No Child Left Behind law failed, district results show.

Math teachers did the worst: Nearly two out of every three failed that exam, while more than half flunked the science test, 43 percent the English exam, and 34 percent the social-studies test.

The results are for 690 of the public school district's 1,346 seventh- and eighth-grade middle school teachers, who took the tests in September and November. Teachers have until June 2006 to take the test and meet the mandate.

Philadelphia teachers failed the test at a far greater rate than those in the rest of the state. Excluding Philadelphia, 77 percent of the 2,905 teachers statewide passed, according to the Pennsylvania Department of Education. One-third of the teachers' statewide who failed work in Philadelphia.

This is very disappointing. Teachers should be able to pass a test if this is the subject they're teaching. They shouldn't be skating on thin ice in terms of content knowledge.

There should be a testing mandate for all teachers. We're holding the kids to higher standards. We need to hold our teachers to higher standards, too.

The federal law specifies that seventh- and eighth-grade teachers need to demonstrate content knowledge in every subject they teach to be considered highly qualified, but it allows each state to set its criteria. That could be the problem.

Pennsylvania requires that teachers pass exams in the subjects they teach. Some other states, such as New Jersey, also offer alternate routes for veteran teachers to meet the requirement, taking into consideration years of experience and college courses as well as outside training in the subject.

Pennsylvania is considering allowing alternate criteria, although no decision has been made. A consideration to eliminate a test to measure teachers is being considered but then the students are expected to pass a test that is not validated where these tests could be bias towards non-white students.

Ross Wiener, a policy analyst at the Education Trust, a Washington-based research and advocacy group, said eliminating the test requirement for teachers did not solve the underlying problem.

"There's a very commonsense statement that teachers cannot teach what they do not know," he said. "Middle school is when students are expected to transition from basic calculations to algebra and advanced math skills. They need teachers with strong content knowledge.

"To eliminate the test is a little bit like shooting the messenger. Obviously these teachers need support," Wiener said.

The testing requirement should matter to parents and they need to fight to keep them and ensure teaching test results are given to the parents. It's like sending people to the front lines in Iraq to fight without the proper weapons. This is an educational war and more money won't fix it. In Pennsylvania, elementary teachers are certified through sixth grade and secondary teachers from seventh through 12th grades. But for schools that span both elementary and secondary grades - middle schools - the state has allowed elementary-certified teachers to teach all grades. Most middle school principals in Philadelphia have preferred elementary-certified teachers to maximize scheduling flexibility; for instance, a math-certified teacher could teach only math, while elementary-certified teachers could teach all subjects.

More than 90 percent of Philadelphia middle school teachers are elementary certified.

The Philadelphia Federation of Teachers says it is pleased that the district plans to offer a test-preparation program for teachers, but questions the fairness of the testing requirement. A test preparation program, are the students given this opportunity? A teacher stated after taking one of the tests that there was stuff on there that she had never seen. She added that some of her colleagues were equally perplexed. When the test was over she stated the teachers put their pencils down and looked at each other with expressions of what was that?

Sound familiar? There is "stuff" guaranteed on the student's tests that have not been validated that students have never seen. However, the students are still held accountable for their scores. Another teacher said one test she took was not an accurate measure of a teacher. Sound familiar? Same argument I gave the Pennsylvania School Board regarding the PSSA test. How can one test measure a student's entire classroom education, experience and knowledge?

Education is just one major issue in this election. Voters must have all the facts in order to make an intelligent selection at the polls. Recently, I was listening to a radio station where they were on the streets asking people who they were going to vote for. It was unbelievable that some people did not know who the Secretary of State was. One guy thought Al Gore was still the Vice President and regarding Kerry; some people didn't have a clue as to who he was. These are some of the voters that will make an important decision on November 2nd. There are many people who do not read the new papers or listen to the news at all. They are completely news illiterate and have no idea what is going on in the world in which they live and don't care to know.

Black Americans unfortunately have followed leadership that has prostituted civil rights for personal gain. They have given the Democrat Party confidence that African Americans will vote Democrat regardless of the candidate policies or remarks.

The distressing part regarding dependent federal programs is, the Democrat Party with the Black Caucus blessings actually feel that Blacks cannot make it on their own without all of the dependent programs. I disagree.

It kind of sounded like when my doctor gave me this 1800- calorie diet and I asked him for an appetite suppressor. He kept saying, Paula you can do it all by yourself. It's going to take some discipline and some work and exercise but you can do it! He went on to tell me that there was no miracle pill and that it won't happen overnight but if you persevere you will make the change in your life and see positive results. I was fine until I walked past the Cherry Cheesecake on my way to the low-fat cottage cheese. I needed help not necessarily funding for a dependent program but rather in my taking the responsibility in making the right choice for good health.

Many people who include African Americans have become dependent on state and federal funded programs. The democrats knew that as long as they maintained dependent programs even though it capitalizes on the insecurities of a race of people, keeping them 'barefoot and pregnant', ultimately keeping them at the back of the bus, the love affair would go on.

The Democrats also maintains the African American support by not voting against affirmative action even though they know the African American for the most part does not benefit from affirmative action the "white" female does. I will admit that there are some situations that we have benefited and should. Affirmative action is to ensure equal opportunities for qualified candidates. It was not developed to fill quotas.

Nearly 40-year history, affirmative action has been both praised and pilloried as an answer to racial inequality. The policy was introduced in 1965 by President Johnson as a method of redressing discrimination that had persisted in spite of civil rights laws and constitutional guarantees. "This is the next and more profound stage of the battle for civil rights," Johnson asserted. "We seek... not just equality as a right and a theory, but equality as a fact and as a result."

President Johnson a democrat in those times of inequality and injustice introducing affirmative action sealed the democrats with a kiss to conquer the African American vote.

The democrats knew that it was a temporary measure to level the playing field focusing in particular on education and jobs. Affirmative action policies required that active measures be taken to ensure that blacks and other minorities enjoyed the same opportunities for promotions, salary increases, career advancement, school admissions, scholarships, and financial aid that had been the nearly exclusive province of whites. From the outset, affirmative action was envisioned as a temporary remedy that would end once there was a "level playing field" for all Americans.

Every girl has more then one suitor. African Americans dated the Republicans in fact Dr. Martin Luther King Jr. was once a Republican. The Democrats were playing hardball to capture the ultimate prize of the African American vote. African Americans felt a choice had to be made which was their biggest mistake. They didn't have to get married to the Democrat Party they should have courted both Democrats and Republicans making them EARN their votes. They could have done this easily by registering independent and fighting for open primaries in every state. The other method could be to split their memberships in both parties still fighting for open primaries in every state. African Americans identified with affirmative action. They began to separate their love affairs between the Republicans and Democrats and placed the major political parties into two categories:

1. Oppose affirmative action equated to promoting discrimination that became the Republicans since some not all Republicans oppose affirmative action.

2. If you were for affirmative action this met that you opposed discrimination practices that became the Democrats after President Johnson introduced the policy.

Let's review some similarity facts:

3. The "white" Democrats and Republicans alike own corporate America and they fund the majority of politicians campaigns both republican and democrats. These are primarily "white" males from both major parties. Corporate America CEO's actually run the country due to funding politician campaigns. These are referred as

being "special interests". This is very dangerous because politicians now represent these "special interests" in order to be re-elected NOT the voters who actually vote them into office. This applies to both major party candidate's democrat and republicans.

4. To give the perception of inclusion there are a small percentage of African American politicians thus created the "Black Caucus". Most of these African American politicians run on the democrat ticket and are usually elected from within minority communities. African Americans usually do not run for elected office in primarily "white" communities. In order to increase the percentage of African American politicians they need to begin to run for elected offices in 'white" communities obtaining the "white" vote on both republican, democrat and even independent tickets. Currently, there are not enough African American politicians to pass any law in this country. In fact you could put all of the minorities together including female politicians and still the 'white" male is the majority in both major parties democrat and republican.

5. The black American became confused when the Democrat Party began to court the African American vote. It has been a long dating game that has turned into an engagement in being taken for granted. It is a marriage that should have never occurred. The African American vote must soon find it's independence in being single not associated to any major political party but rather court each political party making the candidate regardless of their political party affiliation EARN their vote.

Paula Diane Harris

Republicans Fight Back

Going into the 2004 presidential election cycle, Republicans have announced they hope to win 25 percent of the African American vote. Former Speaker of the House Newt Gingrich has great expectations. "If we get African American votes, [the Democrats] are in deep trouble," he told *The Washington Post*. Not just any trouble. *Deep* trouble, he says.

Columnist Jonetta Rose Barras agreed, citing African American voters' growing dissatisfaction with the Democrats that resulted in Arnold Schwarzenegger winning 17 percent of the vote and New York Mayor Michael Bloomberg garnering 22 percent.

The statistics indicate good things for Republicans. According to the oft-cited Joint Center for Political and Economic Studies 2002 political survey, 63 percent of blacks self-identified themselves as Democrats (down from 74 percent in 2000), 24 percent self-identified as Independents (up from 20 percent in 2000) and 10 percent self-identified as Republicans (up from 4 percent in 2000).

Regardless of how blacks self-identify, however, Democrats consistently get 90 percent of African American votes. Why? Years of damage caused by liberal ideology and misinformation pumped into the black community for the past 25 years. Democrats popping up in black church services, civil rights Freedom Fund Dinners, candidate forums where candidates pass out their literature and not made to debate the issues, and annual national conventions such as with the National Association for Colored People

(NAACP), Urban Leagues and other national civil right organizations that draw African Americans plus doing sound bites on urban radio.

Black Americans today many generations have not been educated about the history of the Republican Party and civil rights. Historically, African Americans voted for Republicans because Democrats were blatantly anti-civil rights (and in some ways still are). For example, "radical" Republicans of the 1860s supported slavery's end in America, the Civil Rights Acts of 1866 and 1964 were opposed by Democrats (Senator Robert Byrd participated in a filibuster of the latter) and Jim Crow was a creation of Democrats.

In the 1960s, Democrats blocked school doorways while Republicans pushed de-segregation legislation. In 2004, Democrats continue to block school doorways while Republicans push school choice, the only hope many black parents have to ensure that their kids get a decent education.

So why did African Americans switch from voting for Republicans in large numbers to voting for Democrats? Some say it was President John F. Kennedy's perceived sensitivity to the oppression of minorities that endeared him and the Party to African Americans, and they've been voting for Democrats in droves ever since.

Aside from revisionist history, a more fundamental rift exists between African Americans and Republicans. The concept of limited government—a core Republican principle—is anathema to most African Americans, even wealthy, well-educated ones. Thanks to the handiwork of Southern

Democrats, African Americans continue to turn to the federal government for redress of the slightest racial grievance.

Conservatives have a healthy distrust of the federal government and believe its powers should be limited to only those enumerated in the U.S. Constitution. To most African Americans, however, limited government brings to mind "states' rights," which in turn evokes images of Southern whites and their resentment of federal intervention in local affairs during de-segregation.

The rights of the states are at the heart of a good constitutional republic, but blacks won't easily forget it was the federal government that enforced their civil rights after Reconstruction, got them jobs under the New Deal and protected them from billy clubs, dogs and water hoses in the 1960s. Do you blame them for believing a bloated, central bureaucracy is still savior even in 2004?

It should be emphasized that the federal government is not supposed to have this much control over the people. The U.S. Supreme Court most recently usurped the will of the people by finding a non-existent Constitutional basis for continued race discrimination, although it was legally abolished in 1964. In 1973, they usurped the will of the people by discovering a non-existent "right to privacy" to kill unborn babies. Favoring a strong, forceful central government was once a matter of survival for black's generations ago but no longer.

Given this elemental divide between blacks and Republicans, courting them won't be easy. But the most important advantage Republicans have over Democrats is that Republicans can win elections without the black vote; Democrats can't. So you see this is why Terry McAuliffe Chairman of the Democrat National Committee (DNC) singles out the African American vote painting the picture that they sincerely care about you in realty they only want your vote! Democrats cannot win without the African American vote.

The meantime, African Americans must learn to support candidates regardless of their color, race, or political party affiliation those candidates that: defend our country, support policies that foster economic growth, fight for the sanctity of the family and the dignity of the individual and most importantly those who want to work towards ensuring an equal, quality public education.

Black Americans should be fed up with political lies, fear, resentment and mistrust (and being passed over for leadership positions). It is time African Americans changed their voter registrations to become independents, fight for open primaries in every state giving everyone the right to vote in primaries regardless of their political party affiliation, and to support term limits for every elected official riding our political system of career politicians becoming "Free" from the bondage of empty promises obtaining a taste of real freedom.

The tactics used to court the black American vote is very clear. In this 2004 presidential election the Democrat Party singles out the African

American vote by giving the perception that they are a better choice as a political party then the republicans. A good example of this tactic is Democratic National Committee (DNC) Chairman Terry McAuliffe. Mr. McAuliffe said "the Bush administration's policies have been particularly harmful to the African American community. The African American unelployment rate is almost double the national average. 7.4 million African Americans are without health insurance and millions can barely cover their premiums. African American seniors are struggling to pay for their perscription drugs and students graduating from college are finding themsleves without a job. Democrats are offering real solutions to the very real problems that face the African American communities every day," continued McAuliffe.

Perhaps all the other races registered as Democrats should leave the party since all McAuliffe seems tio advocate for is African Americans?

What McAuliffe won't tell African Americans is that the republicans don't need the African American vote to win elections, democrats do and that is the primary reason why African Americans are singled out by the Democrat Committee.

Democrat Candidates for President

African Americans received the ulitimate "insult" gift from Senator John Kerry in my opinion, the Democrat nominee for President of the United States. Senator John Kerry was looking ahead to November 2004 election, was notable for a wry humor and an all inclusiveness that sought to span races and preferences. "President Clinton was often known as the first black president, "Kerry told the American Urban Radio Network. "I wouldn't ne upset if I could earn the right to be the second".

To add insult, instead of receiving an apology from Senator Kerry, Kerry's spokesman Chad Clanton said: "This was intended as a light-natured remark about President Clinton's strong legacy with African Americans. It is a legacy that John Kerry would like to build upon if elected president. John Kerry has a record of fighting for civil rights and as president he will continue to fight."

Light natured remark as if African Americans are some kind of joke in aspiring to become president of these United States. Our votes are good enough but not our leadership!

In this presidential race there were two African Americans running for president. It doesn't matter wether or not they were your choice of a black candadite to run. The issue is they have the right to run as an American citizen.

I could not understand the nerve of Senator Kerry to make such a statement knowing that two of his rivals for president were African Americans. Talk about verbal abuse!

The African Americans that were running were the Rev. Al Sharpton andCarolyn Moseley Braun. Even though the facts are apparent that neither stood a chance of obtaining the nomination crown regardless of what ticket

they ran on, Senator Kerry's comment nailed the coffin of defeat for any
African American who would dare to try.

Now many would say the reason why neither Rev. Al Sharpton or
Carolyn Moseley Braun wouldn't have a snow balls chance in hell to win
the nomination is because they are black? The same was probably said of
the Rev. Jesse Jackson Sr. when he ran for president. In my opinion that is
not entirely true however, it is a major factor that this country sn't ready for
any minority **to** step into the highest leadership position of this nation. To
have an African American President he or she will have to be able to cross
the color line and attract all races to vote for them. Some African Americans
can only win an election within a minority community but that doesn't
stand true for all African Americans. It has been said that we all look alike
and we are grouped as being the same. This is so far from the truth because
we all defintely do not all look alike. In fact, with the many rainbow of
shades within the African American race we alone look like America and we
defintely do not act or think the same.

Neither the Rev. Al Sharpton made any comment regarding Senator
Kerrys statement even though during the campaign Rev. Sharpton had
alot to say regarding Howard Dean not having hired any blacks within
his administration when governor. In fact, **Howard Dean w**as assailed
for his race record by his rivals for the presidential nomination in the last
democratic debate before the caucuses.

The various Democratic hopefuls took turns chastising Dean, a former
governor of mostly white Vermont, during the Iowa brown and black

Presidential Forum, a two-hour debate focusing on issues important to blacks and Hispanics. It was the third debate in Iowa in eight days. Civil rights activist Al Sharpton forced Dean to acknowledge that no blacks or Hispanics served in his cabinet during 12 years as governor. Rev. Sharpton stated to Dean during a televised debate "While I respect the fact you brought race into this campaign, you ought to talk freely and openly about whether you went out of the box to try to do something about race in your home state and have experience with working with blacks and browns at peer level, not as just friends you might have had in college," Sharpton said.

Dean responded, "I will take a back seat to no one in my commitment to civil rights in the United States of America."

Of course at the time Howard Dean was the frontrunner and had to be taken down at any cost. I am also tired in seeing how some African Americans allow themselves to be used in my as the Rev. Al Sharpton was used to accomplish the task. Does Al Sharpton think any of his democrat political rivals would hire him? If so as what and with what power to make decisions?

Not one civil rights national organization made any comments. Of course the National Association for the Advancement of Colored People (NAACP). The Urban League and the Rainbow Coalition all 501 (C)(3) non-profit organizations even before the Iowa primary, they had their web site links on Senators John Kerry's campaign web site prior to the Iowa Caucus under the title "John Kerry's Community Support". Their web addresses on Kerry's campaign site certainly gives the perception that they supported "Kerry" the candidate and gave the perception that again the Democrats particularly Senator Kerry had the African American support across this nation. The message to black presidential candidates from these civil rights organizations to both major political parties was clear. The divide and conquer won again showing that civil rights organization supposedly fighting for greater opportunities for African Americans would lead the African American vote to elect a 'white' very rich privileged democrat candidate, helping Senator Kerry to earn the right to be the second black president of these United states.

Senator Kerry according to his "light" remark obviously didn't think any of the black candidates could ever earn the right to become president of the United States. Civil Rights organizations confirmed it when they placed their web site links as a support for Senator John Kerry. The Kerry campaign obviously found the price tag to buy the African American vote through the civil rights organizations. To add insult, when I asked Senator Kerry to apologize to every young black American because I felt the remark was offensive, Kerry's spokesman Chad Clanton said: "This was intended as a light-natured remark about President Clinton's strong legacy with African Americans. It is a legacy that John Kerry would like to build upon if elected president. John Kerry has a record of fighting for civil rights and as president he will continue this fight."

Senator Kerry who claims a history in fighting for civil rights should learn to practice respecting the equal rights for all Americans not singling out one group of people such as African Americans, using them only to acquire their votes, taking those votes for granted.

I criticized national civil rights organizations for being silent to Senator Kerry's remark. Evidently they are bondage to their fundraising contributors, which are both democrats as well as republicans. They need to stop, selling out African Americans so cheaply! It's no longer who has the largest memberships, its no longer who is the oldest but it must become about who is the most effective in dealing with civil rights in the 21st century and beyond. Civil rights have stood still since the civil rights movement and many discrimination practices are going unchallenged. Statements such as what Senator Kerry said is just as bad as waving the confederate flag on top of the national capitol dome.

Corporate America and political officials are well aware that our civil rights so called national leaders of today most have cleverly been bought out. The question is does the average African American know and accept it! The leadership that we knew under Dr. Martin Luther King unfortunately is long gone and his leadership has not been replaced.

The following pages are email I received across this nation from all different races regarding the Democrat Party related to African Americans and Senator Kerry's remark about earning the right to become the 2nd black president of the United states.

Chapter V
Black's Don't Read

This piece has been very active in many of the newsgroups and has now apparently been converted to a chain letter. It is possible this has been circulating as a chain letter since 2001. It is reportedly written by an anonymous white man. It was definitely designed to anger blacks. It is an interesting writing piece on a number of levels. Does it perpetuate a racist stereo- type? Without a doubt it does but interestingly it has found a home on a number of black sites and emails. Why? I speculate that this was a piece of satire written by a black person. It lacks many of the race slurs, which would pepper writing like this if it originated with some Neo-Nazi, or KKK member. It says "Blacks DON'T Read" not "Blacks CAN'T Read". It seems to attack the attitudes of a segment of the black population with the intention of angering them into action, rather than belittling them for a lack of intelligence, which is characteristic of hate groups.

Although, there have been many advances by blacks since the civil rights movement of the 1950s and 1960s there is a statistically verifiable lack of reading by a segment of the black population which begins to occur between elementary and high school. Reading scores, which are fairly similar in, lower elementary between blacks and whites take a dip after 2nd grade and by 8th grade are significantly behind white abilities. However, up to the 4th grade children reading for fun seem pretty even between blacks and whites, however after this time blacks read less and less for fun. Since blacks have all the same intellectual capabilities as whites. There must be a

266

cultural explanation for the disparity.

This writing piece you are about to read is recognized by a number of black writers who think that black economic and political power must be promoted through not only the ability to read but also the promotion of it in the black community. The danger of this piece of satire is that few people can recognize a piece of writing as satire when they read it (black or white). As an example, there is a satirical essay still circulating as a chain letter that was written by the Onion (a site devoted to satire) about Harry Potter leading kids into Satanism. This was passed around as a true news report, and despite the obvious exaggerations many people accepted it as fact. Greed, selfishness, and ignorance are not the exclusive domain of blacks. These are evils that find their way into every race, and socio-economic group. You need look no farther than the lily-white Enron and WorldCom executives who showed that these attributes could be found everywhere. The problem is we as black Americans can no longer afford nor should be expected in accepting black leaders who sell us out for their own personal gain exhibiting characteristics of greed and selfishness of their own race.

As a side note, this writing author unknown refers to the racist remarks attributed to Tommy Hilfiger. The comment is patently untrue. Nevertheless, it is a good example of how writing such as this can bolster the perpetuation of a falsehood being circulated in another writing.

This piece could succeed in inspiring some leaders in the black community to try to encourage more involvement in party politics by those in the black community, or to sponsor mentoring programs for "at risk" minorities coming out of high school. However, it could just be read by an ignorant white or black that won't recognize the underline meaning and find this article reinforcement of the racist worldview.

I placed this writing in my book not to entertain you but to shock you into reality. To clearly see yourselves as you are truly seen. To fight each day to make "Blacks Don't Read" untrue as you find courage in your lives to raise your children to become the 1st Black President of these United States of America. To find the courage to rid our race of the sold out leaderships that unlike Rosa Parks and many others who wouldn't give up our seats for justice and equality for their own personal gain.

Love affairs hurt especially when you trusted, were faithful, sacrificed and yes even the loyalty blacks give to the Democrat Party. However, remember time heals all wounds and together we can build bridges that are strong and built with integrity, a bridge that will hold the dreams of our children making them a reality. We cannot any longer remain silent, allowing the voice of civil rights to be chained into bondage. What does "Blacks Don't Read" have to do with being taken serious as a black candidate for president? It has everything to do with us being taken seriously and not taken fro granted. The sad part of the writing regardless of who wrote it many things about it for some blacks in America today and for our civil rights organizations the picture painted fits many shoes within our village. To become the first black president of the United States this is the perception that unfortunately we are up against and it is a perception that we cannot afford to have exist.

Blacks Don't Read- Author Unknown

THEY ARE STILL OUR SLAVES. We can continue to reap profits from the Blacks without the effort of physical slavery. Look at the current methods of containment that they use on themselves: IGNORANCE, GREED, and SELFISHNESS. Their IGNORANCE is the primary weapon of containment. A great man once said, "The best way to hide something from Black people is to put it in a book." We now live in the Information Age. They have gained the opportunity to read any book on any subject through the efforts of their fight for freedom, yet they refuse to read. There are numerous books readily available at Borders, Barnes & Noble, and Amazon.com, not to mention their own Black Bookstores that provide solid blueprints to reach economic equality (which should have been their fight all along), but few read consistently, if at all. GREED is another powerful weapon of containment. Blacks, since the abolition of slavery, have had large amounts of money at their disposal. Last year they spent 10 billion dollars during Christmas, out of their 450 billion dollars in total yearly income (2.22%). Any of us can use them as our target market, for any business venture we care to dream up, no matter how outlandish, they will buy into it. Being primarily a consumer people, they function totally by greed. They continually want more, with little thought for saving or investing. They would rather buy some new sneaker than invest in starting a business. Some even neglect their children to have the latest Tommy or FUBU. And they still think that having a Mercedes, and a big house gives them "Status" or that they have achieved the American Dream. They are fools! The vast majority of their people are still in poverty because their greed holds them back from collectively making better communities. With the help of BET, and the rest of their black media that often broadcasts destructive images into their own homes, we will continue to see huge profits like those of Tommy and Nike. (Tommy Hilfiger has even jeered them, saying he doesn't want their money, and look at how the fools spend more with him than ever before!). They'll continue to show off to each other while we build solid communities with the profits from our businesses that we market to them. SELFISHNESS, ingrained in their minds through slavery, is one of the major ways we can continue to contain them. One of their own, Dubois said that there was an innate division in their culture. A "Talented Tenth" he called it. He was correct in his deduction that there are segments of their culture that has achieved some "form" of success. However, that segment missed the fullness of his work. They didn't read that the "Talented Tenth" was then responsible to aid the Non-Talented Ninety Percent in achieving a better life. Instead, that segment has created another class, a Buppie class that looks down on their people or aids them in a condescending manner. They will never achieve what we have. Their selfishness does not allow them to be able to work together on any project or endeavor of substance. When they do get together, their selfishness lets their egos get in the way of their goal. Their so-called help organizations seem to only want to promote their name without making any real change in their community. They are content to sit in conferences and conventions in our hotels, and talk about what they will do, while they award plaques to the best speakers, not the best doers.

Is there no end to their selfishness? They steadfastly refuse to see that TOGETHER EACH ACHIEVES MORE (TEAM)! They do not understand that they are no better than each other because of what they own. In fact, most of those Buppies are but one or two paychecks away from poverty. All of which is under the control of our pens in our offices and our rooms. Yes, we will continue to contain them as long as they refuse to read, continue to buy anything they want, and keep thinking they are "helping" their communities by paying dues to organizations which do little other than hold lavish conventions in our hotels. By the way, don't worry about any of them reading this letter, remember, 'THEY DON'T READ!!!!'

Civil Rights Organizations their role in the election process

National organizations such as the National Association for the Advancement of Colored people (NAACP), National Urban League, for the most part have become extended families of the Democrat Party even though as 501©(3) they are not to be engaging in political activity. Endorsing candidates is a no non-sense rule of the federal government.

Non-profits are permitted to do education regarding the election process, voter registration, getting out the vote for examples. But placing their web site address on Senator Kerry's Campaign web site under the category of 'Kerry's Community Support" prior to even the Iowa Democrat caucus is over the line.

Of course when Senator Kerry made the comment "he wouldn't be upset to earn the right to be the 2nd black president of the United States when we haven't had the first, these civil right organizations were silent made no public comment. How could they when they were sitting on his web site giving the perception that they had given him the African

American support and vote? In making that statement he certainly didn't feel any of their leaderships were worthy of the office of the president he in his opinion is the best we African Americans can obtain to capture the highest office.

Some may argue and do argue well he's better then Bush. My argument is with that kind of arrogance and attitude he's not good enough!

As Kerry travels across America with African American secret service protecting his life, that's OK but they are not good enough, not better then he to become the first black president of these United States but he's better then Bush!

The concentration has been to get rid of Bush that no concentration has been on what America is going to end up with. This love affair could be worst then the first one.

In my opinion the Democrat Party has prostituted civil rights leaders for the African American vote. Not to get African Americans elected, but to get the career politician (white man and some half sold out black politicians) elected over and over again coming into our communities around election time, making empty promises and then disappearing until the next election.

Some civil rights organizations even have their own awards. One that comes to mind is the Image Awards. We have become so concerned about out starry evening with the rich giving them awards have we forgotten about the issues that our people face everyday? Have we forgot about the field where the memberships of thousands of volunteers working in the community fields across America trying to rid their fields of discrimination, raising our first black president of these United States have the civil rights leaders of today forsaken them?

Oh, I remember now what their reward is. Their reward is the national annual convention. Where they have to worry how they are going to send delegates from their branches because none of the millions of dollars from the national office filters down to the local branches so they can do the work they need to do within their communities. Oh yes, I remember now these people who volunteer and have to send a certain percentage of their fundraising activities to the national office, take vacation from their jobs only to spend black dollars in white hotels and white owned restaurants and store throughout the week going home with the same hopelessness they left with. It is a disgrace and a crime against the civil rights movement. But this is their purpose. Keep your people confused, keep in line for us and we will make sure you have sponsors to keep you personally well paid as well as fringe benefits.

Remember in the beginning of the book when I told you how Africans helped to sell each other to the American slave trade, well the tactic is the same the benefits are different but the tactic is the same and it worked then as it works today.

Many of us know this to be the truth but it's too painful to talk about it. It is painful and it hurts but it is these types of traitors that use their own people that gave Senator John Kerry's republican and democrats alike the nerve to say anything about us and to us without even a notion to apologize. My fellow Americans we have a right to expect better then this!

The role of civil rights organizations is clear in the election process. Deliver the African American vote and we will reward you greatly. The democrats need our votes to win and we will sell out for a McDonald .99 cents menu not realizing with the black dollar we can empower ourselves making them EARN our votes be learning how to distribute our wealth, yes our wealth building our own businesses so we don' t have to beg for pennies in being non-profit. Patronizing our businesses keeping the black dollar within the village.

Martin Luther King Jr. fight was for equality. He wanted us to be able to walk and sit and be waited on in any hotel or restaurant. Remember when he said "don't spend your money where you can't work". It should have been my generation to manage the hotel after the civil rights movement got us into the hotel. It must be our daughters and sons dream to now own it! They're no fear in growing slowly, only in standing still.

Senator Kerry attended the NAACP National Convention this year held in Philadelphia. He walked proudly into the convention center already to hear the applause and be greeted by the NAACP national officials. Kerry, already confident that as he walked out of the convention he had the black vote in his pocket without ever having to earn it. He will waved graciously and gave the perception to those blacks in attendance that with your vote he will make a change in your life never exposing his voting record or standing on any issue that you face everyday of your life.

Senator Kerry is not alone, there are many more from local elected officials all the way up to national level politics. Some even look like you and me only they don't recognize who they really are in the mirror. When they read this chapter they will all deny that they wear these shoes just like Jesus told Judas that he would deny him three times and sure enough he did.

Our first black president of these United States could be sitting in a public school trying to obtain an equal quality education to become the first black president of these United States. The African American white house security that everyday protects Senator Kerry's life and President Bush ready to take a bullet at anytime for their lives may have that dream themselves or hold the dream for their child to become the first black president of these United States. The black soldier who defends our country in Iraq or Afghanistan or another part of the world may have the dream in retuning to America in becoming the first black president of this United States. And yes, every one of these dreams would have "EARNED" the right.

As African Americans pose with grins with Senator John Kerry in the media, can't people tell the difference between when they are being used, not respected only to be taken for granted? It sounds like a bad love affair only the love affair with the Democrats gives the illusion that it really cares about African Americans when in realty it only wants to control your votes. I hold them accountable for their tactics but I blame us for allowing it to happen.

Dr. Martin Luther King Jr. was a Republican and when he was fighting for civil rights he wasn't just fighting against just the Republicans but he fought against all injustices regardless of persons politics. Julian Bond, Chairman of the NAACP should try and follow in King's footsteps.

The worst thing African Americans could have done was place a large majority of their voting power within one political party. The Democrats now feel as though they "own" the black vote. Sounds like slavery all over again. A new master and a new plantation.

A change has got to come........................

Chapter VI
Changing the Guard in Black America

Civil Rights organizations such as the NAACP, Rainbow Coalition and the Urban Leagues epitomized the old and now increasingly discredits black political "leadership" that has so long been the tail on the liberal kite. Fighting the battles of the past, these "leaders" pay little attention to the social tragedies within the black community today. Any criticism of these politicians' own shortcomings, corruption or even crimes are automatically met with charges of "racism."

Worst of all, the black political establishment has become so self-serving that it opposes things urgently wanted and needed by the very minority communities they claim to represent. This fact is very troubling to me and is one of the main reasons I wrote this book. Year after year black conventions rise up across this nation where large membership numbers are used to try and paint a picture of power. But many people know that these memberships are not active within the communities they are to represent. They are only names on apiece of paper, a paid membership with the activity of the member.

Many of these branches and chapters across the nation are enslaved to the local politics placing them in bondage with inadequate leadership. Discrimination issues go unchallenged due to inadequate leadership and people within the communities have lost faith in the very sound of the organizations name. It is time Blacks had a changing of the guard. A good example is education.

No segment of the American population is more in favor of school vouchers than blacks. Yet no political block is more solidly opposed to vouchers than the Congressional Black Caucus.

To put it bluntly, the black establishment is dependent on the liberal establishment in general and the labor unions in particular. The National Education Association, with a substantial bloc of delegates to the Democratic convention, is one of the biggest political contributors to both national and state political campaigns — almost invariably for the Democrats.

The NEA is bitterly opposed to school vouchers, and those who want its support had better be. The NEA is the 800-pound gorilla of the Democratic Party.

State representative Dwight Evans is one of the first black elected officials to break ranks on this issue. He has come out in favor of vouchers. That is why the unions poured in 150 grand to try to defeat him in the Democratic primary in Pennsylvania.

The fact that this massive union effort failed completely when the voters went to the polls is one of the most heartening developments in it and may encourage other blacks in politics to start representing their own communities, rather than the fat cats and rainmakers of the Democratic Party.

It won't happen overnight. But time alone is guaranteed to remove from the scene those generals who keep fighting the last war instead of taking on the battles ahead.

Among the most urgent of those battles is bringing black youngsters up to standard educationally. Instead, black "leaders" are spending their time attacking the tests that show how far behind these students are. In most cases the tests such as in Pennsylvania that are not validated.

These arguments are certainly a lot safer politically than attacking the National Education Association. But it will not help the substandard educational performances revealed by the tests and or how the tests are measured.

Ironically, black students have not always performed as badly on these tests as they do today. Back in 1899, Washington had four academic high schools — three white and one black. On standardized tests given that year, the black high school outperformed two of the three white high schools.

Today, nearly a century later, anyone who even proposed such a thing as a goal would be considered hopelessly utopian. Yet the black high school that held its own in competition with white high schools in 1899 continued to do so for more than half a century.

But that same school cannot come close to doing so today. How could it have succeeded in the era of racial segregation and discrimination, including overcrowded classes, and yet fail miserably today when it has a modern building and the D.C. schools have some of the highest expenditures per pupil in the nation?

Black "leaders" don't even want to ask such questions because it might reveal that they have been barking up the wrong tree for a very long time.

Where is black leadership leading?

Where are all the vocal black "leaders," who are supposedly looking out for their people? "Leaders" who are ready to go ballistic on nationwide TV if Marge Schott or Fuzzy Moeller makes a stupid remark with racial overtones are quiet as mice when AIDS is the leading killer of blacks in the prime years of ages 25 to 34. According to the New York Times, neither the NAACP nor the Urban League has AIDS on its agenda for its national convention this summer.

All this makes sense only if black "leadership" is not about leading black people but extracting what they can from white people and — above all — maintaining themselves in office or in positions of visibility.

One of the truly grotesque acts of black "leadership" occurred earlier this year when District of Columbia Representative Eleanor Holmes Norton led a protest demonstration against school vouchers in Washington. This was in response to a bill sponsored by House Majority Leader Dick Armey and passed by Congress. This bill would have provided 2,000 scholarships for low-income D.C. children to attend private schools.

We can understand why the National Education Association would be bitterly opposed to this and any other voucher legislation that would allow parents to take their children out of the public schools. We can understand why Bill Clinton opposed and ultimately vetoed this bill, since the NEA contributes millions to the Democrats.

It is going to take a strong tummy to deal with the fact that a black "leader" organizes a protest against issues like vouchers when the chief beneficiaries would be black children. What was there to protest? Nobody was going to drag black children out of the public schools, kicking and screaming, and throw them into private schools. It was all up to their parents — and far more parents wanted this opportunity than there were scholarships available.

Poll after poll has shown that blacks are more in favor of school vouchers than any other segment of the population. Yet, time and again, the Congressional Black Caucus and the NAACP opposes vouchers. Are these "leaders" leading blacks or looking out for their own political hides by lining up with the NEA?

Maybe this is just part of coalition politics, where the unions throw their support behind things that the black "leaders" want in exchange for the "Black Leaders" lining up with the unions on the things that the unions want. You heard the saying you scratch my back and I'll scratch yours. The problem with this is the Black people have been sold and they don't realize it. Perhaps this all works out for the politicians and spokesmen involved, but what can the black population as a whole possibly gain that will compensate for condemning another whole generation of their children to rotten public schools?

What also serves the interests of black "leaders," but not of the black community, is their paranoid vision of the world, in which all economic or other disparities are grievances — grievances that could be dealt with only by relying on "leaders" to get goodies for blacks from the government.

This would be a devastating message, even if it were true. It is a catastrophic lie in the light of the facts. The sharpest income and occupational rise of blacks occurred in the 1940s and 1950 — before there was even "equal opportunity" laws, much less "affirmative action."

Far worse than the self-serving actions of black politicians is the vision of the world that they present — especially to the rising generation of young blacks. It is a vision of a world in which everything they don't have is the fault of whites. It is a vision of a future in which their only hope is in changing whites or getting preferences or handouts from the government. This vision is self-destructive for our people and especially for our children. I realize that there is discrimination but Blacks no longer are the only ones who feel the pain of racial injustice and we must stop wearing it on our sleeves. We can fight the injustices in this country and we will win those battles but we can't fight our bad choices in life and continue to label them as discrimination. We have a responsibility in not allowing our life circumstance to dictate our decisions.

With such a vision, why is it surprising that so many students in ghetto schools across the country are afflicted with the suicidal notion that trying to get an education is "acting white"? Many of the very people who promote the liberal vision are themselves appalled at such self-destructive attitudes among young blacks. What is so scary is that it is working.

As Blacks we have got to begin to think for ourselves and not be told how to think by black leaders or political parties. You must refuse to go along with this destructive vision that has been painted. It has succeeded in crippling our family villages allowing blacks to destroy themselves and strip our children of knowing the importance of education. Know that if you can dream it, you can think it, if you can think it you can achieve it. There is no easy way. The only way is hard work earning your way to prosperity achieving the American dream.

By refusing to go along, young black children will at least avoid being played for suckers by a system where the deck has been stacked against them. If a mind is a terrible thing to waste, such a vision is a terrible thing to inflict. Our black children need to see black adults painting a positive picture giving them hope, giving them an example of accomplishment.

Every time I attend a movie I wonder why more black actors and actresses aren't in roles that represent our people in a positive light. Acting movie roles as those played by Denzel Washington, TV roles such as the Huxtables with Bill Cosby and Phylicia Rashad that make you proud to be black. I applaud them for taking roles that do not degrade our people.

To win elections you need a strong campaign manager and ground support. To be able to get good roles for black actresses and actors we need more black writers with vision that write scripts with good English not profanity always making us look like a joke. It is important that actresses who are showcased keep their cloths on making the focus on their talent not their bodies. Black actresses chosen for roles should not all be light and dam near white but also dark skinned showing the diversity within our race. More black producers and directors are needed to make this happen. Without more of these occupations filled by talented blacks with standards many talented African Americans won't be seen on TV or in the movies in talented acting roles.

To pave the way for our country's first Black President we must change our thinking and actions as a people. We must again find the courage to understand our greatness, pick ourselves up and never look back except for an occasional lesson of life. We must acknowledge the importance in setting a positive example for our children being there when they make their mistakes but teaching them how not to make ours. The changing of the guard is not just for our political and civil rights leaders but it is also for our village of families.

This is not the final chapter but must be the beginning of a new book for our people, a new movement in handling civil rights with new techniques and leadership that offer solutions to racism not the continuation of window dressing the issues. Martin Luther King Jr. gave us a dream not to sleep, but to wake up and use the dream to improve our own quality of lives, recognizing we are leaders as the kings and queens that were our African ancestors. We don't have to be content and accept whatever we are told we deserve only to be taken for granted. But rather we must win the battle of equality as we fight for what we know we are worth as Americans, paving the way for generations to come.

The 1ˢᵗ Black President of the United States is born. It is now time we prepare to win the election, to be taken serious!

Epilogue

Today is the beginning of the rest of our lives. The purpose of this book far exceeds the focus only on the 1st Black President but rather how do blacks prepare for this victory? How do blacks obtain respect to be taken serious in America's political structure? How do blacks themselves believe they can aspire to greatness?

Observant that civil rights has been sold to the ghost of Jim Crow by today's leadership. Understanding the political hold on our society that has grabbed on to a perception of masked hope. The acceptance that black votes are being taken for granted recognizing that change is necessary for survival and greater opportunities. This book breaks the truth down for the youngest to understand for generations to come and again solicits courage to deal with a necessary change needed in order to conquer despair.

Blacks don't have to remain hostage in being told they need dependent state and federal funded programs as long term care givers. The chains of oppression can be broken by our life choices. Many blacks are doing the right things but too many are not. Children are a product of their environment and no longer can blame be placed entirely on everyone else for all of the problems. People must begin to take responsibility for the environments they have created..

Martin Luther King Jr. and many others fought to give us the freedom to go into any store or restaurant and to live wherever we choose. He and many others gave up their lives because they thought we were worth ensuring the opportunities we have today. Their sacrifice was not in vain.

Past leaders with high standards such as the late Barbara Jordan set an example and left us a legacy to follow. It is time that we pull together as Americans not as black or white, Republican or Democrat, if not for ourselves for our children.

Civil rights organizations must stop window dressing by having insignificant conventions leading blacks to invest their money throughout the week into white hotels and businesses instead of strategically planning how to increase black owned businesses ensuring economic development.

It is time for the black village to stop allowing politicians to come into their neighborhoods at election time making more empty promises just to get elected and I mean all politicians! Politicians are aware that blacks have become content and complacent.

This book is about finding courage to continue the dreams of prosperity. It's about not being afraid in growing slowly but only afraid in standing still.

My dreams are different then Martins and they should be as he told us, he wouldn't get to the promise land with us but he left us a map. This book must be a constant reminder of not what everyone else can do for you but what people can achieve for them-selves.

I understand the difficulty in accepting change but we can no longer afford to pursue and follow the wrong paths accepting the wrong advice from black leaders who are blinded by self-gain. Different paths will be chosen and we will even disagree but we must cease in being disagreeable allowing the divide and conquer mentality to win. People are like a plants either shriveling or developing. It should be impossible for us to stay the same however, some fight up against the inevitable.

This book is not a dream but it is pages of self- development to make dreams of the past become realities of tomorrow.

It is time that the village of African Americans awake to realization that we have some housecleaning chores to do.

Our African ancestors had so much less but did so much more and we have so much more but are doing so much less. Don't allow the Jim Crow ghost to enslave your minds that are destroying the village. Sports and R&B- Hip Hop music has gotten many blacks out of the ghetto but understand that reading a book and being able to comprehend and articulate what you have read will keep you out! Blacks must increase educational achievements and until this has been accomplished, the cries of the slaves that have long ago fulfilled their purpose will not be heard.

Free at last, free at last, thank God almighty we are free at last...............

ENDNOTES

Chapter 1

1. Brown v. Board of Education
   Issue: Racial Segregation in Public Schools
   Thurgood Marshall with James Nabrit Jr. and George E.C. Hayes
   after their victory in the Brown v. Board of Education case before
   the Supreme Court, May 17, 1954.

2. Fourteenth Amendment of the Constitution

3. Section 8 of the United States Constitution

4. H J RES 114

5. Article II of the Constitution

6. White House Historical Association with Cooperation National
   Geographic Society.

7. New Book of Knowledge

8. BECOMING A PRESIDENTIAL NOMINEE
   . *By Stephen J. Wayne*

9   Black Information Link March 23, 2004

10. Noble *e* Museum

11. The African American Journey of Barbara Charline Jordan

12. Ebonics Translator

Chapter II

1.   Congressman Jesse Jackson 2004 Kerry VP Press Release

Chapter V

2.   Blacks Don't Read

Bibliography

Branch, Taylor, *Parting the Waters: America in the King Years, 1954–63* (Simon & Schuster 1988).

Burns, Stewart, ed., *Daybreak of Freedom: The Montgomery Bus Boycott* (Univ. of N.C. Press 1997).

Halberstam, David, *The Children* (Random House 1998).

Kluger, Richard, *Simple Justice: The History of Brown v. Board of Education and Black America's Struggle for Equality* (Knopf 1976).

Powledge, Fred, *Free at Last? The Civil Rights Movement and the People Who Made It* (Little, Brown 1991).

Sitkoff, Harvard, *The Struggle for Black Equality, 1954–1992,* rev. ed. (Hill & Wang 1993).

Van Deburg, William L., *New Day in Babylon: The Black Power Movement and American Culture, 1965–1975* (Univ. of Chicago Press 1992).

Amy, Douglas, *Real Choices—New Voices: The Case for Proportional Representation in the United States* (1993).

Bibby, John F., *Politics, Parties, and Elections in America*, 3d ed. (1996).

Butler, David, *British General Elections since 1945*, 2d ed. (1995).

Fredman, L. E., *The Australian Ballot* (1968).

McGillivray, Alice, and Scammon, Richard, *America at the Polls*, 2 vols. (1995).

Norris, Pippa, ed., *Elections and Voting Behavior* (1998).

Aldrich, John H., *Why Parties?* (1995).

Beck, Paul A., and Hershey, Marjorie R., *Party Politics in America*, 9th ed. (2001).

Budge, Ian, and Keman, Hans, *Parties and Democracy: Coalition Formation and Government Function in Twenty States* (1993).

Cox, Gary W., *Making Votes Count*

Wayne, Stephen J., Road to the White House: The Politics of Presidential Elections; Politics of American Government

Adams, Russell, *Great Negroes Past and Present*, pp. 106-107. Chicago, Afro-Am Publishing Co., 1963.

Bennett, Lerone, Jr., *What Manner of Man: A Biography of Martin Luther King, Jr.* Chicago, Johnson, 1964.

I Have a Dream: The Story of Martin Luther King in Text and Pictures. New York, Time Life Books, 1968.

About the Author

Paula Diane Harris founded the Andrew Young National Center for Social Change, Inc. (AYNCSC) in 2003. The center is the first for-profit minority owned corporation that is dedicated to effecting social change through the economic empowerment of businesses and communities in the nation.

Paula Diane Harris began her career in civil rights as a volunteer for the National Association for the Advancement of Colored People (NAACP) for nearly eight years beginning as a Youth Advisor. In conjunction to her daughter's leadership as youth president together they developed the most admired and effective NAACP youth council in Pennsylvania. Ms. Harris was then elected to the Executive Committee of the adult branch, then elected 1st Vice President and finally elected president in 2000.

Among numerous accomplishments as president, Paula Diane Harris a registered independent voter was responsible under her leadership of the local NAACP Branch in establishing the first NAACP office in the City of Harrisburg in the branch's forty- year plus history and developed their first web site to increase public knowledge for the local branch office.

Ms. Harris a working, divorced, single parent also worked for many years in the health insurance business as she raised her only child Rogette Nicole Harris who has been the inspiration of her life.

Ms Harris currently fulfills many public speaking engagements across the country specializing in civil rights in the 21st century, legislative and political topics and is the spokesperson for the Andrew Young National Center for Social Change Inc. as President and CEO. Her signature" There is only one race and that is the human race" Ms Harris is currently working on a series of writings about 21st century political slavery and how civil rights lost its voice.